W9-BPJ-325

TABLE OF CONTENTS

ASSESSMENTS

Grammar Assessment

I. **Identify the parts of speech (Adjective, Adverb, Conjunction, Noun, Preposition, Verb)**

<u>Bob</u> <u>was</u> a good man. I <u>used</u> to converse with him every morning <u>before</u> I ran to

¹ ² ³ ⁴
work. <u>We</u> would stop at the Dunkin' Donuts, which was <u>next</u> to the Starbucks. I

⁵ ⁶
<u>preferred</u> Dunkin' Donuts <u>because</u> I loved to get a <u>delicious</u> Boston Crème <u>with</u> my

⁷ ⁸ ⁹ ¹⁰
coffee. He loved our time at the Dunkin' Donuts because he loved our <u>conversations</u>,

¹¹
<u>and</u> I did too.

¹²

He told me of the years he had <u>spent</u> as a CIA agent, <u>scouring</u> the world for the

¹³ ¹⁴
"baddies," as he so <u>simply</u> put it. <u>Watching</u> his eyes <u>intently</u>, I swore I could see him

¹⁵ ¹⁶ ¹⁷
reliving those <u>lurid</u> scenes in front of me. <u>Taking</u> me back with <u>him</u> was his gift. Each

¹⁸ ¹⁹ ²⁰
morning, I left right <u>at</u> the climax <u>of</u> a tale, <u>so</u> the ending would dance <u>perpetually</u> in

²¹ ²² ²³ ²⁴
my mind's eye through the remainder of the day.

One morning, <u>however</u>, the stories <u>stopped</u>. I'll <u>always</u> miss Bob. I go <u>to</u> the

²⁵ ²⁶ ²⁷ ²⁸
Starbucks now.

1. Noun
2. Verb
3. ~~adverb~~ Verb
4. Preposition
5. Noun
6. Preposition
7. Verb
8. Conjunction
9. adjective
10. preposition
11. Noun
12. Conjunction
13. Verb
14. Verb

15. adverb
16. Verb
17. adverb
18. adjective
19. ~~verb~~ Noun
20. Noun
21. Preposition
22. Preposition
23. Conjunction
24. adverb
25. ~~Conjunction~~ adverb
26. Verb
27. adverb
28. Preposition

II. **Write the singular possessive and the plural possessive of the following nouns:**

Noun	Singular Possessive	Plural Possessive
1. dog	dog's	dogs'
2. author	author's	authors'
3. parent	parent's	parents'
4. friend	friend's	friends'
5. teacher	teacher's	teachers'
6. person	person's	people's
7. man	man's	men's
8. woman	woman's	women's
9. boss	boss's	bosses's
10. James	James'	James's
11. child	child's	Children's
12. rapper	rapper's	rappers'

III. **Examine the sentences below. Determine whether the underlined punctuation is correct. If not, provide a correct alternative.**

1. The Smiths, who were my favorite family—always brought brownies.

2. The dessert was so delicious; I just wanted to eat all of it.

3. There are several things I need you to get, including toilet paper and CHEEZ-Its.

4. Katy Perry loves to sing loudly, and with energy.

5. It's important that you turn the lights off, so you do not waste electricity.

6. When the dog finally barked, I could tell he was hungry.

7. I had fun with you yesterday: Broncos all the way!

8. Okay, that's enough. No more punctuation questions for me.

9. He says, he wants more of them.

10. "I'm done!" I told him.

IV. **Underline the Main subject and the Main verb and determine if they agree in number (singular with singular / plural with plural). If they don't, fix the problem.**

1. The class of students is happy.

2. A number of people believes you should stop running for office.

3. The number of voters is seven.

4. One of the earliest musicians of the Middle Ages are here to talk to you.

5. Suddenly, my family and I are unable to find the royal jewels.

6. There is a schedule to be discussed and a table of contents to be examined.

7. Each of us think that you took the cookie from the cookie jar.

8. Each of them knows it's a lie.

9. Hey bud, the row of books are starting to get too heavy.

10. The group of chickens cross the road to get away from the first chicken.

V. **Underline the verbs and identify their tenses.**

1. The movie was so good.

2. I have enjoyed action movies my entire life.

3. By the time Brad Pitt had become a star, I was hooked on all his movies.

4. Yesterday, for example, I sang a whole anthem about Brangelina.
5. Some people say I am obsessed.

6. At least I will have spent my life loving rather than losing.

7. After all, I used to be bored.

VI. **Determine if the sentences employ the idiomatically proper word choices. If not, fix them!**

1. The cheeseburger ~~effected~~ *affects* me so much that I started to cry.

2. I cannot believe food can have that ~~affect~~ *effect*!

3. Yes it can! It always illicits such a craving in me.

4. Wow. Well, I've always just rather spent money on books ~~then~~ *than* on food.

5. Then, I should buy you books for Christmas.

6. No way. You don't need to get me anything for Christmas. I'm against gift giving on ~~principal~~ *principle*.

7. Why? You think the love behind gifts is all one big allusion?

8. No! I believe in the love. It just seems like its a waste of time buying things for each other.

9. Whose going to ever stop buying though?

10. No one. I think it maybe worth writing about though.

Math Assessment

NUMBERS AND OPERATIONS

Properties of numbers and basic operations

1. Complete the chart below. Check whether the numbers are rational, integers, and/or positive numbers. You may check more than one box for each number.

	Rational	Integer	Positive
1	✓	✓	✓
−2	✓	✓	
−2.3	✓		
−2.345	✓		
$^1/_2$	✓		✓
$^2/_{27}$	✓		✓
π			✓
13.356	✓		✓
3^2	✓	✓	✓
$\sqrt{23}$			✓
0	✓	✓	

2. Place the following numbers in the correct order from least to greatest:

0.25, $^2/_5$, $\sqrt{9}$, -100, π, 0.245, -0.01, 2^3

$-100, -0.01, 0.245, 0.25, \frac{2}{5}, \pi, \sqrt{9}, 2^3$

3. Let a number followed by Ψ indicate the greatest prime factor of that number. (For example, 12Ψ = 3, because the prime factors of 12 are 2 and 3, and 3 is the greatest of these.) Evaluate the following:

A. 25Ψ = 5
B. 42Ψ = 7
C. 30Ψ 5
D. 700Ψ = 7

4. Complete the chart below by finding the greatest common factor (GCF) and the least common multiple (LCM) of the number groups:

	GCF	LCM
4 and 16	4	16
2 and 3	1	6
30 and 42	6	210
10, 25 and 35	5	350

5. Complete the chart below by matching the numbers to their opposites (additive inverses) and reciprocals (multiplicative inverses):

Number	Opposite	Reciprocal
4	-4	$\frac{1}{4}$
15	−15	$\frac{1}{15}$
$\frac{2}{3}$	$-\frac{2}{3}$	$^3/_2$
$-^9/_7$	$\frac{9}{7}$	$-\frac{7}{9}$

6. Simplify:

   A. $(2 + 3) \cdot 3^2$ *45*

   B. $3 \cdot 4 + 10 \div 2$ *24*

   C. $5^3 \div 6$ *19*

   D. $\sqrt{12/(2 \cdot 2) + 3^3/27}$ $\sqrt{3+1}$ ②

7. Simplify:

   A. $|-2|$ 2

   B. $|5 - 4|$ 1

   C. $\sqrt{81}$ 9

   D. $\sqrt{18}$ $3\sqrt{2}$

8. Without a calculator, put a check in each column that is a factor of the number in each row:

	1	2	3	4	5	6	8	9	10
2568	✓	✓	✓	✓		✓	✓		
5265	✓		✓		✓				
3233	✓								
7830	✓	✓	✓		✓	✓			✓
4936	✓	✓		✓			✓		

9. Based on the table in question 8, what is the remainder when each of the numbers in the first column is divided by 7? (You may use a calculator.)

10. Simplify:

    A. $3/5 + 4/15$ $\frac{9}{15} + \frac{4}{15} = \boxed{\frac{13}{15}}$

    B. $9/5 - 3/4$

    $\frac{36}{20} \cdot \frac{15}{20} = \boxed{\frac{21}{20}}$

11. Simplify:

    A. $2/5 \cdot 2/7$ $\boxed{\frac{4}{35}}$

    B. $3/5 \div 9/10$

    $\frac{3}{5} \times \frac{10}{9} = \frac{30}{45} = \frac{6}{9} = \boxed{\frac{2}{3}}$

12. In your math class, there are 3 girls for every 2 boys. $2:3 = 12:x$

    A. If there are 12 boys, how many girls are there? 18

    B. If there are 15 total students, how many are girls and how many are boys?

    $9 \text{ girls}, 6 \text{ boys}$

13. Simplify the complex fraction:

    $$\frac{1/2 - 3/10}{2/12 + 1/3}$$

    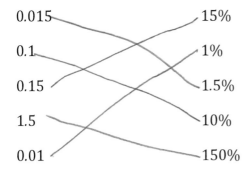

    $\left(\frac{1}{2} - \frac{3}{10}\right) \div \left(\frac{2}{12} + \frac{1}{3}\right)$

    $\left(\frac{5}{10} - \frac{3}{10}\right) \div \left(\frac{1}{6} + \frac{2}{6}\right)$

    $\frac{2}{10} \div \frac{3}{6}$ $\frac{1}{10} \times \frac{2}{1} = \frac{2}{10} = \boxed{\frac{1}{10}}$

14. Match each decimal to its correct percent form:

    0.015 — 15%

    0.1 — 1%

    0.15 — 1.5%

    1.5 — 10%

    0.01 — 150%

15. Compute:

    A. $0.6 \cdot 0.3 = 0.18$

    B. $1.41 + 1.5 = 2.91$

    C. $25\% + 50\% = 75\% = 0.75$

16. What number is 20% of 80?

$$\frac{80}{.2}$$
$$16.0$$

(16)

17. You are owed $30, but you only receive $27. What percent of what you owed do you actually receive?

$$\frac{27}{30} = \frac{x}{100}$$

$$\frac{2700 = 300x}{30} \qquad x = 90$$

(90%)

18. You decided to give 60% of your old stuffed animals away to charity, so you donated 15 of your old toys. How many toys did you have before you donated any?

$$\frac{60}{100} = \frac{15}{x}$$

$$1500 = 60x$$

$$x = 25$$

(25)

19. Complete the chart by converting from scientific notation to numerical form and vice-versa:

Scientific Notation	Numerical Form
1.234×10^3	1234
-6.5×10^5	-0.650000
-3.0×10^{-2}	-0.030
$8.901 \cdot 10^{-3}$	0.008901

20. Simplify:

   A. $(3 \cdot 10^2) + (4 \cdot 10^1) =$ $300 + 40 = 340$

   B. $(6.2 \cdot 10^6) \div (2.0 \cdot 10^4) =$ $\dfrac{6,200,000}{20,000} = 310$

21. Which of the following statements is logically equivalent to "if p, then q?"

   A. If q, then p.
   B. If not p, then not q.
   C. If not q, then not p.

22. Paula Positive tells her son, Contra, that he will definitely get a cookie before bed if he finishes his homework. Which of the following is logically equivalent?

   A. If he gets his cookie, Contra will finish his homework.
   B. If Contra doesn't finish his homework, he'll get no cookie.
   C. If Contra goes to bed cookie-less, he hasn't finished his homework.
   D. Any cookie Contra gets, he gets because he finished his homework.

ALGEBRA

Exponents and Radicals

23. Perform the indicated operations and simplify:

A. $a^3 \cdot a^4 \cdot a^{-2} = a^5$

B. $\dfrac{q^5}{q^3} = q^2$

C. $(b^3)^2 = b^6$

D. $\dfrac{\dfrac{a^2b}{cd^{-2}} \cdot \dfrac{acd^2}{b^5}}{\left(\dfrac{ab^{-2}c^3d}{a^0}\right)^2} = $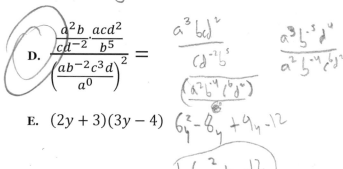

E. $(2y+3)(3y-4)$ $6y^2 - 8y + 9y - 12$

$$\boxed{6y^2 + y - 12}$$

24. Indicate whether each statement must be true or false for all numbers $x, r,$ and s.

A. $(-x)^2 = -x^2$ False

B. $(-x)^3 = -x^3$ True

C. $(\sqrt{x})^3 = x^{3/2}$ True

D. $(\sqrt[3]{x})^2 = x^{2/3}$ True

-8 E. $(-\sqrt{x})^3 = x^{-3/2}$ False

F. $(r+s)^2 = r^2 + s^2$ False

25. Factor:

    A. $6p + 24 = (p+4)6$

    B. $q^2 - 3q - 10 = (q-5)(q+2)$

    C. $2x^2 + 11x + 14 = (2x+7)(x+2)$

    D. $3x^2 - 10x + 7 = (3x-7)(x-1)$

    E. $9a^2 - 12a + 4 =$

    F. $x^8 - 8x^4 + 16 =$

    G. $h^2 - 64 =$

    H. $9m^2 - 121 =$

    I. $t^3 - 3t^2 + 4t - 12 =$

    J. $2x^3 + 8x^2 - 4x - 16 =$

26. True or False?

    A. $2x^2 - 6x + 3$ has only one root. False

    B. $2x^2 - 8x + 5$ has two rational roots. False

Solving Equations

27. You add 4 to a number and multiply the sum by 3. Your result is 27. What was your original number?

$$3(x+4)=27$$
$$3x+12=27 \quad 3x=15 \quad \boxed{x=5}$$

28. One half of the difference between a number and 5 is 11.5. What is the number?

$$x-5 = 23 \quad \boxed{x=27}$$

29. You enter your jar of jelly beans into a contest, and you win! As a prize, you get a second jar of jelly beans with twice as many jelly beans as are in your original jar. Your excited aunt sends you an extra 50 jelly beans in a box as a celebratory gift. Between the two jars and the box, you now have 500 jelly beans total. How many did you start with?

$$x+2x+50 = 500$$
$$3x = 450 \quad \boxed{y=150}$$

30. Three consecutive even integers add up to 24. What is the smallest of the integers?

$$x+x+2+x+4=24$$
$$3x \quad 3x+6=24 \quad \boxed{x=6}$$
$$3x=3x=18$$

31. On a drive to school 15 miles away, you travel an average speed of 25 miles per hour for the first 3 miles, an average speed of 50 miles per hour for the next 10 miles, and then back to 25 miles per hour for the last 2 miles. How long does it take you to get to school?

$$7.2 + 12 + 4.8$$

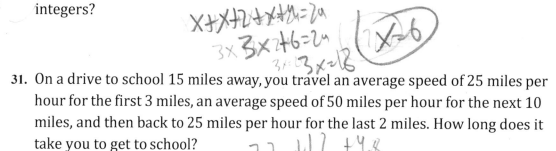

$$12+12 = \boxed{24}$$

32. Solve for x:

A. $|x + 2| - 3 = 8$ $\boxed{\{-13, 9\}}$

B. $x^2 - 4x = x - 6$

$$x^2-5x+6$$
$$(x-3)(x-2)$$
$$\{3,2\}$$

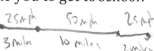
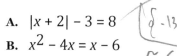
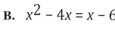

$$\frac{25}{?} = \frac{3}{x} \quad 60$$

$$180$$

$$\frac{50}{60} = \frac{10}{x} \quad 600 = 50x$$

$$\frac{25}{60} = \frac{2}{x} \quad 120 = 25x$$

33. Solve and sketch a number line graph indicating the range of r:

A. $4 - 3r \leq -5$ $-3r \leq -9$

$3r \geq 9$

$r \geq 3$

B. $\frac{r-4}{-2} < 1$

C. $|r + 2| > 3$

D. $|4r - 1| \leq 2$

34. Solve for x and y:

A. $x + y = 10$ $x = 10 - y$
$\quad\; x + 4y = 7$

$x + y = 10$

$x + 4y = 7$

$3y =$

$10 - y + 4y = 7$ $x = 11$

$3 = -3y$ $y = -1$
$\qquad y = -1$

B. $3y + 4x = 2$ $9y + 12x = 6$
$\;\;\;\; 5y + 3x = 3$ $-20y - 12x = -12$

$\qquad\qquad\qquad\quad \dfrac{-11y = -6}{-11}$ $y = \dfrac{6}{11}$

$3 \cdot \frac{6}{11} + 4x = 2$

35. There are 40 children in a class of boys and girls. When one fifth of the boys and one third of the girls show up for class, there are only 10 children present. How many girls are there in the class when all students are present?

Let $x =$ # of boys

Let $y =$ # of girls

$x + y = 40$ $x = 40 - y$

$\dfrac{1}{5}x + \dfrac{1}{3}y = 10$

$\dfrac{40y}{5} + \dfrac{1}{3}y = 10$

$\dfrac{120 - 3y}{15} + \dfrac{5y}{15} = 10$

$150 = 120 + \text{th}$ $\dfrac{120 - 3y + 5y}{15} = 10$

$\boxed{15}$

$2y = 30$ $y = 15$ $\dfrac{120 + 2y}{15} = 10$

FUNCTIONS

Function Notation and Tabular Functions

36. Solve:

A. $f(x) = 3x + 7,$ $\quad f(3) = 16$

B. $f(t) = t^2,$ $\quad f(c) = 16.$ $\quad c = 4, -4$

C. $f(x) = x^3 - 3,$ $\quad g(x) = \frac{x+4}{2},$ $\quad g(f(2)) =$

D. $h(t) = 2t + 2,$ $\quad j(t) = \frac{t^3}{4},$ $\quad h(j(c)) = 6,$ $\quad c =$

E. If a_c^b is defined as $a + b \cdot c$, then $2_5^3 - 1_3^2 = 17 - 17 = 0$

x	f(x)	g(x)	h(x)
-5	-3	5	3
-3	-2	3	2
-1	-1	1	1
0	0	0	0
1	1	1	-1
3	2	3	-2
5	3	5	-3

37. Given the table above, evaluate:

A. $f(-3) = -2$

B. $10 - g(-5) = 5$

C. $3h(3) = -6$

D. $5 + f(g(-5)) = 4$

E. $-g(h(-5)) = 3$

F. $f(f(f(g(h(f(0)))))) = 0$

G. $1 - h(1 + f(-h(-5))) = 0$

H. Given the table above, why can't you find $g(f(3))$?

Thought

Students	Pencils
10	15
20	30
30	45

38. The above graph represents how many pencils are necessary for a class of a certain size. How many pencils will be necessary for a class of 26 students?

$$\frac{10}{15} = \frac{26}{X}$$ 39

Depth	Oxygen
50	100
100	50
200	25

39. The above graph describes a relationship for oxygen concentrations at deeper and deeper depths. At a depth of 1000 units, approximately, what will be the oxygen concentration?

5

40. The force of gravity varies inversely as the square of the distance betwen two objects. If the distance is increased three-fold, will the force of gravity increase or decrease? By what factor?

Decrease three fold.

STATISTICS AND PROBABILITY

Statistical Analysis

41. Complete the chart by identifying mean, median, mode, and range of the data sets provided:

	Mean	*Median*	*Mode*	*Range*
1, 1, 2, 3, 8	3	2	1	7
2, 2, 2, 3, 3, 3	2.5	2.5	{2,3}	1
−3, 7, 9, 11	6	8		14

42. Tammy is 60 inches tall, Timmy is 65 inches, and Tommy is 66 inches. I don't know how tall Sarah is, but I know that the mean of all four people's heights is 64 inches. How tall is Sarah?

$\boxed{65\text{ in}}$

$$\frac{60 + 65 + 66 + x}{4} = 64$$

$$191 + x = 256$$

$$x = 65$$

43. For your end-of-year research project, you recorded how many times in a row people sneezed. You recorded 30 people over the course of a week. Your results are recorded in the table below.

Sneezes in a row	Frequency
1	8
2	18
3	3
4	1

A. How many sneezes did you hear in total?

B. What are the mean, median, and mode number of sneezes in a row?

2.5   2.5   N/a

C. If you were to draw a line graph of this data, which of the following would the graph's shape most resemble?

    i. A bowl
    ii. A mountain
    iii. A descending hill
    iv. An ascending ramp

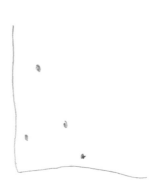

44. A bag contains 3 white marbles, 2 red marbles, and 4 blue marbles. If I choose a marble at random from the bag, what is the probability that the marble will be white?

$\frac{1}{3}$

45. I roll a regular 6-sided die 2 times. What is the probability that I roll a 4 both times?

$\frac{1}{12}$

46. There are 4 extra-credit problems on a test, and each question has 5 answer choices. How many different complete answer keys are possible for this section?

625

47. Clara has three children. She has returned from an overseas business trip with five different t-shirts that she thought her children might like as gifts. If she gives one shirt to each child, in how many different possible ways can she give out the shirts?

48. A square with a perimeter of 8 cm lies entirely within a square with a perimeter of 20 cm. If I throw a dart and it lands somewhere inside the larger square, what is the possibility that it will land in the smaller square?

49. Using wooden posts and planks, Steve will build a decorative fence aruond a 20-foot by 20-foot garden. He will place one post every 4 feet, and then he will connect them with three planks between each neighboring pair of posts. He will leave an open space between a single pair of posts, by not placing planks between them, in order to create an entrance to the garden. How many posts and planks does Steve need in order to build his fence?

PLANE AND SOLID GEOMETRY

Plane Geometry: Triangles and Squares

50. Complete the chart below by indicating if the given triangle is acute, obtuse, right, isosceles, and/or equilateral. You may check more than one box for each item. Images are drawn to scale.

	Acute	Obtuse	Right	Isosceles	Equilateral
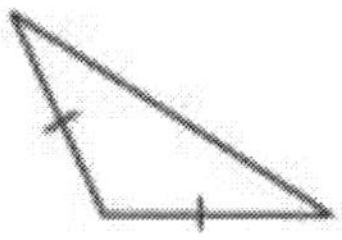		✓		✓	
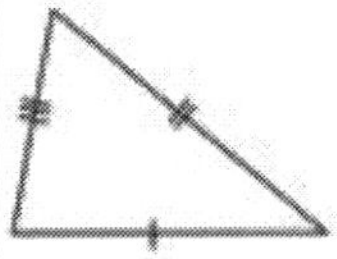	✓			✓	
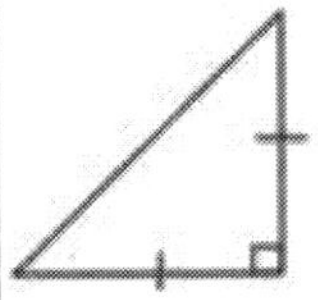			✓	✓	
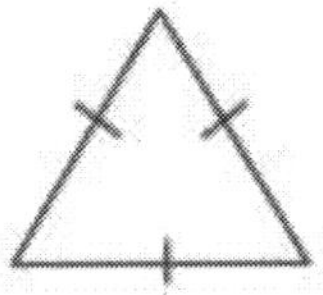	✓			✓	✓

51. Find side *a* and angle *A* in the triangle below.

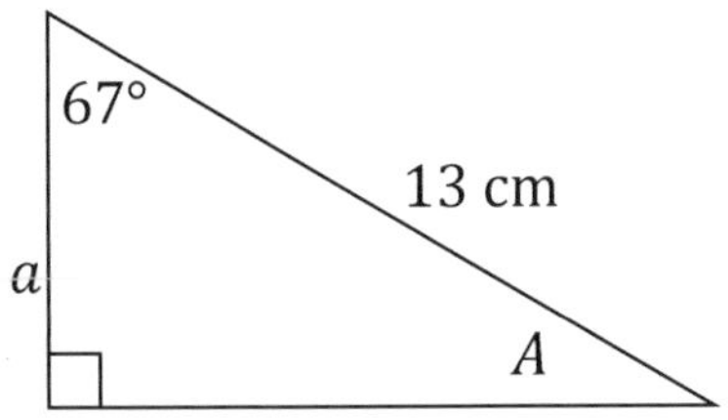

SOHCAHTOA

52. What is the area of triangle *ABC* below?

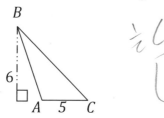

$\frac{1}{2}(5\times6)$

15

53. Find the measure of angle *x*, below.

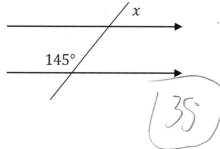

145°

$35°$

54. Right triangle *ABC* is similar to triangle *DEF*. Suppose $2(CA) = DF$ and $AB = CB = 2$.

A. Find the measure of angle *DEF*. 45

B. Find the length of the longest side of triangle *DEF*. 8

C. Find the ratio of the measure of angle *ACB* to the measure of angle *DFE*. 1:1

D. Find the ratio of the measure of angle *ACB* to the measure of angle *DEF*. 2:1

55. In equilateral triangle *ACE*, *B* is the midpoint of segment *AC*, and *D* is the midpoint of segment *CE*. *AE* = 10.

A. Find *BD*. 5

B. Find the ratio of the perimeter of triangle *BCD* to the perimeter of triangle *ACE*. 1:2

C. Find the ratio of the area of triangle *ACE* to the area of triangle *BCD*.

12.5:100

12.5:100

56. One side of a square is also the hypotenuse of a 30 – 60 – 90 triangle. If the diagonal of the square is 1 cm, find the length of the shortest side of the triangle.

57. One side of an equilateral triangle is also the side of a square. The equilateral triangle has $\frac{\sqrt{3}}{2}$ square feet. Find the length of the diagonal of the square.

58. What is the area of the circle below? What is its circumference?

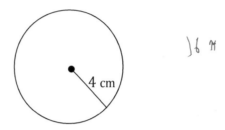

16 π

59. Jacob's pie chart has a radius of 18 inches and a blue sector denoting the 80% of Americans who live in cities. What is the area of the sector?

60. What is the length of an arc subtended by a central angle of 10 degrees on a circle of radius 5 cm?

61. If line *AD* and a circle with center *C* are tangent at point *B* on the circle, what is the degree measure of angle *ABC*?

62. What is the area of the parallelogram below?

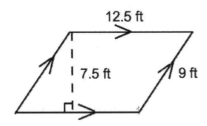

12.5 ft

7.5 ft   9 ft

63. Given the parallelogram below, can lengths *AB* and *BC* be determined? If so, what are they? If not, why not?

No You need more info, more sels.

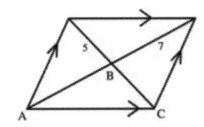

5   7

B

A   C

64. Given the rhombus below, can angles *x* and *y* be determined? If so, what are they? If not, why not?

$x = 40$

$y = ?$

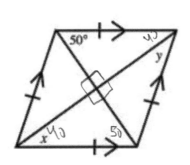

50°   40

y

x 40   50

65. If the area of the trapezoid below is 64, find the height h.

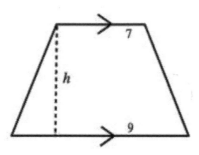

66. What is the measure of an exterior angle of any n-sided polygon?

$$\tfrac{360}{n} \, (n-2)$$

67. What is the measure of each interior angle of any regular n-sided polygon?

$$\frac{360}{n-2}$$

68. What is the sum of the measures of the interior angles of any n-sided polygon?

$$360$$

69. Find the surface area and volume of a 3-cm-by-4-cm-by-5-cm rectangular prism.

$V = 60$

SA

70. Find the length of the longer diagonal you can fit inside a 3-cm by 4-cm by 5-cm rectangular prism.

71. Find the surface area and volume of a right cylinder of height 15 in. and radius 5 in.

72. If you slice a right cylinder parallel to its bases, what is the shape of the cross section you obtain? If instead you slice it perpendicular to its bases, what is the shape of the cross section you obtain?

parallel (Circle)

⊥: Rectangle

COORDINATE GEOMETRY

Lines and Slope

73. What is the slope of a line passing through the points $(-4, 5)$ and $(2, 6)$?

$\frac{6-5}{2+4} = \boxed{\frac{1}{6}}$

74. What is the slope of the line given by $2x - 3y = 5$?

$y = -\frac{2}{3}x - \frac{5}{3}$

$-3y = -2x + 5$

$3y = 2x - 5$

$\boxed{\frac{2}{3}}$

75. What are the slopes of the lines $y = 7$ and $x = -2$?

$y = 7 \boxed{0}$

$x = -2 \boxed{\text{undefined}}$

76. What are the x- and y- intercepts of the line given by $y = \frac{-5}{2}x + \frac{3}{4}$?

$y = \boxed{\frac{3}{4}}$

$x = \boxed{\frac{3}{10}}$

$\frac{3}{4} = -\frac{5}{2}x$ $\frac{3}{4} \cdot \frac{2}{5}$

$\frac{6}{20}$

77. Provide an equation of a line that is parallel to the line given in question 74.

$y = \frac{2}{3}x + 3$

78. Provide an equation of a line that is perpendicular to the line given in question 76.

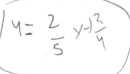

$y = \frac{2}{5}x + \frac{3}{4}$

79. Find the equation of the line of slope -3 which passes through the point $(-4, -5)$.

$y = -3x + b$

$-5 = 12 + b$

$b = -17$

$\boxed{y = -3x - 17}$

80. Find the midpoint of the points $(\sqrt{2}, -\sqrt{3})$ and $(\sqrt{2}, \sqrt{3})$

$$\left(\frac{2\sqrt{2}}{2}, 0\right) \quad \frac{\sqrt{2}+\sqrt{2}}{2}, \frac{\sqrt{3}-\sqrt{3}}{2}$$

81. If the midpoint of Point A and (–3, 6) is (1, 4), find the coordinates of Point A.

$(5, 2)$

82. Find the distance between the two points in question 80.

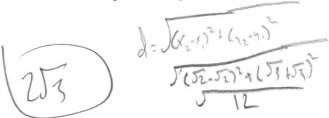

$2\sqrt{3}$

$$d = \sqrt{(x_2-x_1)^2 + (y_2-y_1)^2}$$

$$\sqrt{(\sqrt{2}-\sqrt{2})^2 + (\sqrt{3}+\sqrt{3})^2}$$

$$\sqrt{12}$$

83. A bee leaves the beehive in search of nectar. The bee first flies 20 meters west, then 60 meters north, then 110 meters east before finally flying straight back to its hive. What is the total distance the bee flew?

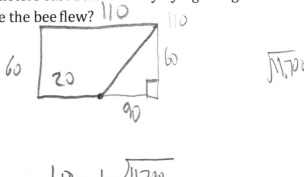

$$190 + \sqrt{11700}$$

$$190 + 10\sqrt{117}$$

$$190 + 30\sqrt{13}$$

$$\left(190 + 30\sqrt{13}\right)$$

108.16

84. Describe what happens to the graph of an original function $f(x)$ if its equation is changed in each of the following ways:

A. $f(x)+3$ I+ will be 3 units higher on the y-axis

B. $f(x)-5$ 5 units lower on the y-axis

C. $f(x+1)$

D. $f(x-7)$

E. $-f(x)$

F. $f(-x)$

G. $2f(x)$

H. $\frac{1}{2}f(x)$

I. $f(4x)$

J. $f(\frac{1}{4}x)$

K. $-5f(-5x)-5$

ADVANCED TOPICS

Trigonometry

85. The hypotenuse of right triangle ABC measures 7 units long, and $\angle ABC$ measures 40 degrees. Find the measures of the other sides and angles of the triangle.

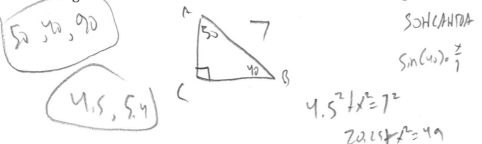

50, 40, 90

4.5, 5.4

SOHCAHTOA

$\sin(40) = \frac{x}{7}$

$4.5^2 + x^2 = 7^2$

$20.25 + x^2 = 49$

$x = 28.75$

86. You are standing exactly 100 feet from a 105-foot-tall building, and your eyes are exactly 5 feet above the ground where you stand. What is your angle of elevation as you look to the top of the building?

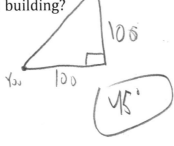

You   100   100

45°

87. How many degrees are in a circle? How many radians are in a circle?

360°, 2π radians

88. How many radians are equivalent to 60 degrees? How many degrees are equivalent to 2 radians? Keep your answers in exact form.

89. Simplify the following expressions (assume $0 \le \theta \le \pi/2$):

A. $\dfrac{\cot \theta \sec \theta}{\csc \theta}$

B. $3(\cos \theta)^2 + 3(\sin \theta)^2 =$

C. $\sqrt{1 - (\cos \theta)^2 - (\sin \theta)^2} =$

90. If $\cos \theta = -\dfrac{1}{2}$ and $\pi < \theta < \dfrac{3\pi}{2}$ then find $\sin\theta$, $\tan\theta$, $\csc\theta$ $\sec\theta$, and $\cot\theta$.

91. Determine the amplitude and period of the graph of the function $y = 3\sin\left(\dfrac{x}{2} + 1\right)$.

92. Find the 19th term of the arithmetic sequence beginning with −4, 7, 18, 29, 40, 51, 62, 73, 84, 95, 106,
117, 128,
139, 150, 161
172, 183

194

93. Find the 9th term of the geometric sequence beginning with 2, −6, 18 ... 54, 162, 488

1 3 1 2 2

94. Find the 100th digit after the decimal in the decimal representation of $5/7$.

95. What is the common difference of the arithmetic sequence in question 92?

$n + 11$

96. What is the common ratio of the geometric sequence in question 93?

1 · −3

97. What is the sum of the integers from 1 to 100, inclusive?

5050

98. What is the sum of the multiples of 5 from 5 to 55, inclusive?

330

Logarithms

99. Convert the following logarithmic equations into their equivalent exponential forms:

    A. $\log_2 32 = 5$

    B. $\log 0.0001 = -4$

    C. $\ln 1 = 0$

100. Convert the following exponential equations into their equivalent logarithmic forms:

    A. $2^{10} = 1024$

    B. $7^2 = 49$

    C. $5^{-3} = \dfrac{1}{125}$

101. Condense the following expressions down into a single term with a single logarithm:

    A. $\log 5 + \log 10$

    B. $\log_5 60 - \log_5 15$

    C. $3\ln 4 - \ln 6 + 2\ln 2$

102. Solve for x:

    A. $x^7 = 10$

    B. $7^x = 10$

    C. $\log_x 8 = 3$

    D. $\log_2 x + \log_2(x+1) = 1$

103. What is the radius of the circle given by the equation $(x+2)^2 + (y+6)^2 = 23$?

$\sqrt{23}$

104. What is the center of the circle given by the equation $(x-5)^2 + (y+7)^2 = 100$?

$(5, -7)$

105. What is the equation of a circle centered at $(1, -2)$ and with a circumference of 6π?

$(x-1)^2 + (y+2)^2 = 9\pi^2$

106. Find the axis of symmetry and vertex of the parabola with equation
$y = 3x^2 + 2x - 1$.

107. Find the x- and y-intercepts of the parabola given in question 106.

108. If the axis of symmetry of a certain parabola is $x = 5$ and one of the zeros of the parabola is -7, find its other zero.

Complex Numbers

109. If $a = 3 + 4i$, $b = 7 - 2i$, $c = -4i$, and $d = 3$, compute the following:

A. $a + b - c - d =$

B. $abcd =$

C. $\dfrac{bc + d}{a}$

D. the complex conjugates of each of a, b, c, and d.

110. Compute i^{79} from the repeating pattern of the powers of i.

111. Find the roots of the polynomial $x^2 + 6x + 10$.

$$\frac{-6 \pm \sqrt{6 \cdot 40}}{2}$$

112. If a quadratic polynomial has $3 + 2i$ as one of its roots, what must its other root be?

Grammar Assessment Answer Key

I.

1. Noun
2. Verb
3. Verb
4. Preposition
5. Noun
6. Preposition
7. Verb
8. Conjunction
9. Adjective
10. Preposition
11. Noun
12. Conjunction
13. Adjective (Past Participle)
14. Adjective (Present Participle)
15. Adverb
16. Adjective (Present Participle)
17. Adverb
18. Adjective
19. Noun (Gerund)
20. Noun
21. Preposition
22. Preposition
23. Conjunction
24. Adverb
25. (Conjunctive) Adverb
26. Verb
27. Adverb
28. Preposition

II.

	Noun	*Singular Possessive*	*Plural Possessive*
1.	dog	dog's	dogs'
2.	author	author's	authors'
3.	parent	parent's	parents'
4.	friend	friend's	friends'
5.	teacher	teacher's	teachers'
6.	person	person's	people's
7.	man	man's	men's
8.	woman	woman's	women's
9.	boss	boss's	bosses'
10.	James	James's	Jameses'
11.	child	child's	children's
12.	rapper	rapper's	rappers'

III.

1. The Smiths, who were my favorite family—always brought brownies.

   Incorrect: Change to em-dash

2. The dessert was so delicious, I just wanted to eat all of it.

   Incorrect: Change to either a period or a semi-colon.

3. There are several things I need you to get: including toilet paper and

   CHEEZ-Its.

   Incorrect: No punctuation is necessary.

4. Katy Perry loves to sing loudly, and with energy.

   Incorrect: No punctuation is necessary.

5. It's important that you turn the lights off, so you do not waste electricity.

   Correct

6. When the dog finally barked; I could tell he was hungry.

   Incorrect: Change to comma

7. I had fun with you yesterday: Broncos all the way!

   Correct

8. Okay, that's enough. No more punctuation questions for me.

   Correct

9. He says, he wants more of them.

   Incorrect: No punctuation is necessary.

10. "I'm done!" I told him.

    Correct

IV.

1. The **<u>class</u>** of students **<u>is</u>** happy.

    Correct match!

2. A **<u>number</u>** of people **<u>believes</u>** you should stop running for office.

    Correct match!

3. **<u>The number</u>** of voters **<u>is</u>** seven.

    Correct match!

4. **<u>One</u>** of the earliest musicians of the Middle Ages **<u>are</u>** here to talk to you.

    "Are" should be **"is."**

5. Suddenly, **<u>my family and I are</u>** unable to find the royal jewels.

    Correct match!

6. There **<u>is</u>** a **<u>schedule</u>** to be discussed and a **<u>table</u>** of contents to be examined.

    "Is" should be made **"are."**

7. **<u>Each</u>** of us **<u>think</u>** that you took the cookie from the cookie jar.

    "Think" should be **"thinks."**

8. **<u>Each</u>** of them **<u>knows</u>** it's a lie.

    Correct match!

9. Hey bud, the **<u>row</u>** of books **<u>are</u>** starting to get too heavy.

    "Are" should be **"is"**

10. The **group** of chickens **cross** the road to get away from the first chicken.

    "Cross" should be **"crosses."**

V.

1. The movie **was** so good.

   Past

2. I **have** enjoyed action movies my entire life.

   Present Perfect ("enjoyed" is past participle)

3. By the time Brad Pitt **had** become a star, I **was** hooked on all his movies.

   Pluperfect ("become" is past participle)

   Past in passive voice ("hooked" is past participle)

4. Yesterday, for example, I **sang** a whole anthem about Brangelina.

   Past

5. Some people **say** I **am** obsessed.

   Present; Present

6. At least I **will have** spent my life loving rather than losing.

   Future Perfect ("spent" is past participle)

   Note: "loving" and "losing" are not verbs!

7. After all, I **used to be** bored.

   Imperfect; Infinitive

VI.

1. The cheeseburger **effected** me so much that I started to cry.

   affected

2. I cannot believe food can have that **affect**!

   effect

3. Yes it can! It always **illicits** such a craving in me.

   elicits

4. Wow. Well, I've always just rather spent money on books **then** on food.

   than

5. Then, I should buy you books for Christmas.

   Correct!

6. No way. You don't need to get me anything for Christmas. I'm against gift

   giving on **principal**.

   principle

7. Why? You think the love behind gifts is all one big **allusion**?

   illusion

8. No! I believe in the love. It just seems like **its** a waste of time buying things

   for each other.

   it's

9. **Whose** going to ever stop buying though?

   Who's

10. No one. I think it **maybe** worth writing about though.

    may be

Math Assessment Answer Key

1.

	Rational	*Integer*	*Positive*
1	X	X	X
−2	X	X	
−2.3	X		
−2.345	X		
$^1/_2$	X		X
$^2/_{27}$	X		X
π			X
13.356	X		X
3^2	X	X	X
$\sqrt{23}$			X
0	X	X	

2. -100   -0.01   0.245   0.25 $^2/_5$ $\sqrt{9}$ π 2^3

3. A. 5   B. 7   C. 5   D. 7

4.

	GCF	*LCM*
4 and 16	4	16
2 and 3	1	6
30 and 42	6	210
10, 25 and 35	5	350

5.

Number	Opposite	Reciprocal
4	-4	$1/4$
15	−15	$1/15$
$2/3$	$-2/3$	$3/2$
$-9/7$	$9/7$	$-7/9$

6. A. 45   B. 24   C. 20r5   D. 2

7. A. 2   B. 1   C. 9   D. $3\sqrt{2}$

8.

	1	2	3	4	5	6	8	9	10
2568	X	X	X	X		X	X		
5265	X		X		X			X	
3233	X								
7830	X	X	X		X	X		X	X
4936	X	X		X			X		

9. 2568: 6   5265: 1   3233: 6   7830: 4   4936: 1

10. A. $13/15$ B. $21/20$

11. A. $4/35$ B. $2/3$

12. A. 18   B. 9 girls, 6 boys

13. $2/5$

14. 1.5%   10%   15%   150% 1%

15. A. 018   B. 291   C. 75%

16. 16

17. 90%

18. 25

19.

Scientific Notation	Numerical Form
1.234×10^3	1234
$-6.5 \cdot 10^5$	-650000
-3.0×10^{-2}	-0.030
$8.901 \cdot 10^{-3}$	0.008901

20. A. 340   B. 310

21. B. if not p, then not q

22. A. If he gets his cookie, Contra will finish his homework.

   B. If Contra doesn't finish his homework, he'll get no cookie.

   C. If Contra goes to bed cookie-less, he hasn't finished his homework.

   Any cookie Contra gets, he gets because he finished his homework.

23. A. a^5

   B. q^2

   C. b^6

   D. $ac^{-6}d^2$

   E. $6y^2 + y - 12$

24. A. False

   B. True

   C. True

   D. True

   E. False

   F. False

25. A. $6(p + 4)$

   B. $(q - 5)(q + 2)$

   C. $(2x + 7)(x + 2)$

   D. $(3x - 7)(x - 1)$

   E. $(3a - 2)^2$

   F. $(x^2 + 2)^2(x^2 - 2)^2$

   G. $(h + 8)(h - 8)$

   H. $(3m + 11)(3m - 11)$

   I. $(t^2 + 4)(t - 3)$

   J. $2(x^2 - 2)(x + 4)$

26. A. False
    B. False

27. 5
28. 28
29. 150
30. 6
31. 24 minutes
32. A. -13,9
    B. 2,3

33. A. $r \geq 3$
    B. $r > 2$
    C. $r < -5 \text{ or } r > 1$
    D. $\frac{-1}{4} \leq r \leq \frac{3}{4}$
34. A. $x = 11, y = -1$
    B. $x = \frac{1}{11}, y = \frac{6}{11}$
35. 15

36. A. 16
    B. -4,4
    C. $\frac{9}{2}$
    D. 2
    E. 10
37. A. -2
    B. 5
    C. -6
    D. 8
    E. -3
    F. 0
    G. 0
    H. f(3) is 2, but g(2) is not given

38. 39
39. 5
40. Decrease by a factor of 9

41.

	Mean	*Median*	*Mode*	*Range*
1, 1, 2, 3, 8	3	2	1	7
2, 2, 2, 3, 3, 3	2.5	2.5	2 and 3	1
−3, 7, 9, 11	6	8	none	14

42. 65 inches

43. A. 57

B. mean: $\frac{57}{30}$, median: 2, mode: 2

C. A mountain

44. $\frac{1}{3}$

45. $\frac{1}{36}$

46. 625

47. 60

48. $\frac{4}{25}$

49. 20 posts, 57 planks

50.

	Acute	*Obtuse*	*Right*	*Isosceles*	*Equilateral*
		X		X	
	X				
			X	X	
	X			X	X

51. 5 cm, 23 degrees

52. 15

53. 35 degrees

54. A. 90

    B. $4\sqrt{2}$

    C. 1:1

    D. 1:2

55. A. 5

    B. 1:2

    C. 4:1

56. $\sqrt{2}/_4$ cm

57. 2 ft

58. Area = 16π square cm, Circumference = 8π cm

59. 243π

60. $\frac{5\pi}{18}$ cm

61. 90 degrees

62. 93.75 square feet

63. Yes. $AB=7$, $BC=5$

64. Yes. 40 degrees and 40 degrees

65. 8

66. $\frac{360}{n}$

67. $180 - \frac{360}{n}$

68. $180(n-2)$

69. SA = 94 square cm, Volume = 60 cubic cm

70. $5\sqrt{2}$ cm

71. SA = 200π square inches, Volume = 375π cubic inches

72. Circle, Rectangle

73. $\frac{1}{6}$

74. $\frac{2}{3}$

75. 0 and undefined

76. $\frac{3}{10}$ and $\frac{3}{4}$

77. $y = \frac{2}{3}x + C$

78. $y = \frac{2}{5}x + C$

79. $y = -3x - 17$ or $y + 5 = -3(x + 4)$

80. $(\sqrt{2}, 0)$
81. $(5,2)$
82. $2\sqrt{3}$
83. 280 meters

84. A. Shifted 3 up
   B. Shifted 5 down
   C. Shifted 1 to the left
   D. Shifted 7 to the right
   E. Reflected across the x-axis
   F. Reflected across the y-axis
   G. Stretched vertically by a factor of 2
   H. Shrunk vertically by a factor of 2
   I. Shrunk horizontally by a factor of 4
   J. Stretched horizontally by a factor of 4
   K. Reflected across the x-axis, stretched vertically by a factor of 5, reflected across the y-axis, shrunk horizontally by a factor of 5, shifted 5 down.

85. Sides: 7sin40 units, 7cos40 units
   Angles: 50 degrees, 90 degrees
86. 45 degrees
87. 360 degrees, 2π radians
88. $\frac{\pi}{3}$ radians, $\frac{360}{\pi}$ degrees
89. A. 1
   B. 3
   C. 0
90. $\sin\theta = -\frac{\sqrt{3}}{2}$ $\tan\theta = \sqrt{3}$ $\csc\theta = -\frac{2\sqrt{3}}{3}$ $\sec\theta = -2$ $\cot\theta = \frac{\sqrt{3}}{3}$
91. Amplitude = 3, Period = 4π

92. 194
93. 13122
94. 2
95. 11
96. -3
97. 5050
98. 330

99.   A. $2^5 = 32$
       B. $10^{-4} = 0.0001$
       C. $e^0 = 1$

100.   A. $\log_2 1024 = 10$
       B. $\log_7 49 = 2$
       C. $\log_5 \frac{1}{125} = -3$

101.   A. $\log 50$
       B. $\log_5 4$
       C. $\ln \frac{128}{3}$

102.   A. $\sqrt[7]{10}$
       B. $\log_7 10$
       C. 2
       D. 1

103. $\sqrt{23}$

104. $(5, -7)$

105. $(x-1)^2 + (y+2)^2 = 9$

106. $x = -\frac{1}{3}, (-\frac{1}{3}, -\frac{4}{3})$

107.   -1, $\frac{1}{3}$ and -1

108.   17

109.   A. $7 + 6i$
       B. $264 - 348i$
       C. $\frac{-127 - 64i}{25}$
       D. $3 - 4i, 7 + 2i, 4i, 3$

110. $-i$

111. $-3 + i, -3 - i$

112. $3 - 2i$

CHAPTER 1: GRAMMAR

English Strategies

INTRODUCTION

The majority of questions on the ACT English section deal with grammar, including diction, syntax, and punctuation. However, a fair number of questions on the ACT deal with meaning instead. This book will help prepare you for these more complex questions as well as provide you with some general guidelines for tackling all of the questions.

FORMAT

The English section lasts 45 minutes and consists of 5 passages of 15 or so questions each for a total of 75 questions. The passages, and the questions within them, do not increase in difficulty with the number of the questions, so you should do all the questions in the order in which they appear. The questions feature a variety of topics, from rules of grammar to expository analysis.

APPROACHES

Read the Passage

You should treat the English section as an exercise in editing. If you were editing a friend's paper for school, you would read it through, trying to understand its main argument, and marking it up along the way whenever you found an error. You will need to follow this twofold approach here. As you do so, keep the grammatical errors in the front of your mind, as the majority of questions will deal with them, but also keep in the back of your mind the larger considerations of theme and structure.

Always Read the Entire Sentence

Students will often try to determine whether the underlined portion of a sentence is correct or not based only on the words that immediately surround it. But unless you read the entire sentence, there is no way to be certain. Always read the entire sentence before you decide whether the underlined portion is correct.

Timing

There are two types of questions: those that deal with grammar and those that deal with meaning, context, etc. In general, you should be spending about 20 seconds on the former, and up to 45 seconds on the latter. As this suggests, the latter require more time. In your practice exams, get used to using two different speeds for these two types of questions.

If It Isn't Broken, Don't Fix It

Keep in mind that "NO CHANGE" is very frequently the correct answer. If you've read something through carefully (paying attention to punctuation), and it sounds okay to you, you should strongly consider choosing NO CHANGE. However, keep in mind the next approach:

Check For Redundancy

Remember that the ACT doesn't only test your knowledge of grammar, but of *meaning*. For example, consider the sentence, "Every year, scientists all along the Amazon carefully measure and record the annual rainfall." Grammatically, there is nothing wrong with this sentence. However, it is *redundant* because it unnecessarily repeats an idea: "Every year" and "annual" mean the same thing, so there is no need to include both. If you have read through a sentence, and it sounds okay, before choosing NO CHANGE, pause and ask yourself, "Is it redundant?"

Less Is More

If you've decided that there's something wrong with a sentence and that you're not going to be choosing NO CHANGE, *always check the shortest answer first*. More often than not, the answer choice that features the fewest words and least punctuation is the correct one.

Be Specific

Some questions will ask you what would be the best addition to a sentence or paragraph to fulfill a specified purpose. In general, the answer choice that provides the most specific detail will be the correct one.

Unnecessary Vs. Irrelevant

Some questions will ask whether or not a sentence or part of a sentence should be omitted. If the portion or sentence contains information that is not absolutely necessary, but is related to the main idea of the paragraph or passage (for example, something that provides descriptive detail), leave it in. However, if the text distracts from the main idea, or awkwardly breaks up the sentence that comes before and after it, omit it.

Transitions

Some questions will deal with transition words, (such as "therefore," "however," "furthermore," etc.), which provide a connection from one idea to another. When dealing with this type of problem, many students find it useful to read the portion before, *skip the transition words*, and then read what follows, asking themselves whether the two statements agree with each other or if they contain some kind of contrast. If the two statements agree, the correct answer will contain "connecting" words, such as "therefore," "so," "because," etc. If the two statements contain contrast, the correct answer will contain contrast words, such as "but," "however," "although," "on the other hand," etc.

For example, consider the following two sentences, with the transition words underlined, and the answer choices below:

Everyone had heard what a kind and generous man John was. <u>However,</u> they were all eager to make his acquaintance.

A. NO CHANGE

B. On the other hand,

C. That notwithstanding,

D. Therefore,

Because the statement that comes before the transition word ("however") and the statement that comes after it are both positive, it is safe to assume that the transition word should show agreement. The only choice to do so is the correct answer, D. Even when this strategy will not eliminate all of the incorrect answer choices, it will usually knock out at least two.

Where Does This Belong?

Some questions will ask you to determine where a sentence should be placed, either within the entire passage or within a given paragraph.

- o ***Within the Entire Passage:*** Look for a close connection between the content of each paragraph (especially the sentences that surround the suggested area of placement) and that of the sentence you are placing. The paragraph with the strongest connection will be the correct one.

- o ***Within a Given Paragraph:*** Keep an eye out for words such as "the," "this" "these," "that," "those," and any pronouns. These words are used to refer to something that has already been discussed, and very frequently on the English section, to something that has been discussed in the sentence that should come immediately before the one in question.

  For example, a question might ask you where within a paragraph you should place the sentence "After we discovered the river's source, we decided that we could camp there for the night." Because the sentence uses the word "the" to describe the river's source, chances are excellent that this sentence should be placed immediately after whatever sentence also refers to the river or its source.

Was the Author Successful?

Some questions, especially those that come at the very end of a passage, will ask you to determine whether or not the author did a good job of writing on a specific topic. For example: "Suppose the writer had chosen to write a brief essay about the history of the automobile. Would this essay successfully fulfill the writer's goal?" Even though these questions might seem somewhat daunting at first because of their scope, they are usually quite easy. Simply go back and re-read the title of the essay and the topic sentence of each paragraph. That should give you an adequate sense of whether the author fulfilled his or her goal.

Keep It Moving

You have less time per question on the English section than on any other. If you find yourself spending too much time on a particular question, take an educated guess and move on. It's a good idea to circle the ones you're not sure about, so that you can go back and check over them at the very end if you have the time to do so. However, keep in mind the next approach:

Don't Flip-Flop

On the math section of the test, you can check at least some of your answers with the help of your calculator. But on the English, you have no such tool to fall back on, so trust your first instincts for two reasons: 1. First guesses are more often correct than second-guesses; and 2. Going back to change answers takes up valuable time that could be used to work on other problems. Unless you see that you have made a clear mistake, go with your first choice.

Grammar Guide

INTRODUCTION

Grammar, especially that of English, can be a frustrating subject. There are a seemingly endless number of rules, not to mention the exceptions to these rules. The good news is that the ACT and SAT only test a small fraction of the rules and ask the same kinds of questions almost every time. Once you have familiarized yourself with the terms and tactics below and worked with your academic coaches to solidify these concepts, you'll be in good shape to take on almost any question the test-makers might throw at you.

PARTS OF SPEECH

In order to understand why certain words are used in certain contexts, it is essential to first learn the different categories of words and their respective functions. Make sure that you fully comprehend the terms below:

Nouns

A noun is a person, place, thing, or idea. For example, in the sentence "Sometimes grammar can be confusing," "grammar" is the noun.

Verbs

Verbs denote actions. For example, in the sentence "Practice makes perfect," "makes" is the verb. Keep in mind that existing is an action, and therefore "is," "are," "was," "were," "will" (and all other forms of "to be") are verbs. A verb may be either singular (such as "eats," as in "he eats") or plural (such as "eat," as in "they eat").

 Watch Out! Words such as "is," "are," "was," "were," "will be," "would have" and so on are all forms of "to be," and, although they might not seem very "active," are still verbs. In fact, a large number of problems on the ACT and SAT refer to these words (called "linking verbs") and it is therefore essential to keep an eye out for them.

 Watch Out! Most words that end in "-ing," which some might think are verbs, are actually either nouns (called "gerunds") or adjectives (called "present active participles"). For example, in the sentence "All her studying paid off," "studying" is a gerund, a kind of noun that describes an action. In the sentence "We crossed the raging waters," "raging" is describing the noun "waters," and is therefore a kind of adjective, known as a present active participle. Note that the word "present" here refers to the ongoing nature of an action; these participles can be used in conjunction with *any* tense, not just the present.

Adjectives

These are description words. Specifically, they describe, or modify, nouns or other adjectives. For example, in "the big bad wolf," the adjectives "big" and "bad" both describe the noun "wolf." In "the bright red coat," however, the adjective "red" describes the noun "coat," while the other adjective, "bright," describes "red."

Adverbs

These words often end in "-ly" are used to describe verbs, adjectives, and other adverbs. For example, in "he quickly realized," the adverb "quickly" describes the verb "realized." In other words, an adverb that modifies a verb tells how or on what basis an action is performed. In "she was deeply sorry," the adverb "deeply" modifies the adjective "sorry"; in "he ate incredibly slowly," the adverb "incredibly" modifies the other adverb "slowly."

 Watch Out! Only adverbs can modify verbs; adjectives cannot. For example, in the sentence "It was the most wonderful designed machine he had ever seen," "wonderful" should be changed to "wonderfully."

 Watch Out! Although most adverbs end in "-ly," not all of them do—for example, many adverbs of time, such as "always," "never," "often," and "sometimes."

Pronouns

These words stand in for a noun. For example, in the sentence "The police asked for Tom's cooperation, but he refused," "he" is a pronoun that stands in for the noun "Tom." The noun a pronoun stands in for is known as its antecedent. So in the above sentence, the antecedent of "he" is "Tom."

Prepositions

These are words that show the relationships, spatial and otherwise, between terms. Common prepositions include "above," "by," "for," "in," "of," "outside," "with," and so on. For example, in the sentence "He had to decide between the ACT and SAT," "between" is a preposition.

 Watch Out! The preposition "between," like the adjective "both" and the phrase "at once," denotes a plural, and is always followed by two items joined with an "and." For example, the sentence "He had to choose between ice-cream or cake," is incorrect because "or" here denotes a singular thing (see subject-verb agreement, below), and should be changed to "and."

Conjunctions

These words are used to connect items. Common conjunctions include "and," "but," "if," "since," "so," "with," "yet," and so on. In the sentence "She narrowed down the answer to A or D," "or" is a conjunction.

Interjections

These are words that add emotion to a sentence, but do not affect its overall grammar. Interjections often come at the beginning of the sentence and are usually directly followed by either an exclamation point or a comma. In the sentence "Well, this sure is news to me," the word "well" is an interjection.

SENTENCE STRUCTURE

Subjects and Main Verbs

Every sentence must contain at least one subject and one main verb. The main verb indicates the action that is taking place (even if it is a subtle action such as existing, denoted, for example, by the verb "is"). The subject, which is always a noun, is whoever or whatever is performing the action. In the sentence "I catch the ball," "I" is the subject and "catch" is the verb. In the sentence "The ball hit me," "ball" is the subject and "hit" is the verb. There is no limit to how long the subject of a sentence can be. In the sentence "the person who exemplifies all the best characteristics of compassion, generosity, and wisdom and takes the time to show me how much she cares is my mother," the full subject is "the person who exemplifies all the best characteristics of compassion, generosity, and wisdom and takes the time to show me how much she cares."

Independent Clauses

Independent clauses contain at least one subject and main verb and can stand on their own. Every full sentence is either an independent clause or a collection of independent clauses that have been joined together. For example, "She wants to do her best" is an independent clause (and one full sentence), while "She wants to do her best, and she works hard every day" is still one sentence, but contains two independent clauses joined by the comma and the conjunction "and."

Dependent Clauses

These statements also contain at least one subject and verb, but cannot stand alone because they do not contain a complete thought. For example, the statement, "because he had saved his work for the last minute" is a dependent clause.

 Watch Out! Unless it is being used as part of a question, the word "who" serves to introduce a dependent clause, and any verb that appears within a dependent clause cannot be the main verb of a sentence. Note that the words "which" and "that" also often serve to introduce dependent clauses. When a dependent clause stands alone, and is finished with a period, it is known as a **sentence fragment**. For example: "Our kind uncle who visits us each year, bringing us gifts of every kind." This is a sentence fragment, for while it does contain a subject, "our kind uncle," there is no main verb, because the verb "visits" appears inside a dependent clause that is introduced by "who." Also note that coordinating conjunctions, such as "because," "when," "whereas," and "although," (see coordinating conjunctions, below) also introduce dependent clauses.

 Private Prep Tactic: When appropriate, change dependent verbs to main verbs by deleting "who," "which," or "that." For example, we can easily correct the sentence fragment above by simply deleting the word "who": "Our kind uncle visits us each year, bringing us gifts of every kind."

GRAMMATICAL RULES

The topics below list grammatical rules, and their corresponding errors, in order from most to least common. Because the same kind of error will often be tested multiple times in the course of one test, it is imperative that you learn to recognize the rules and errors consistently, regardless of the topic of a particular sentence or paragraph.

Category	Incorrect	Correct
Subject-Verb Agreement (Inverted Syntax)	"Just over the next hill is the house and the lake."	"Just over the next hill *are* the house and the lake."
Subject-Verb Agreement (Prepositional Phrase)	"The sounds of the birds, dogs, and her only pet cat wakes her every morning."	"The sounds of the birds, dogs, and her only pet cat *wake* her every morning."
Subject-Verb Agreement (Collective Singulars)	"A number of scientists is excited to attend."	"A number of scientists *are* excited to attend."
Agreement and Sequence of Tenses	"I have finished but she did not."	"I have finished but she *has* not."
Verb Moods	"If I was there, I would celebrate with you."	If I *were* there, I would celebrate with you."
Verb Voices (Active vs. Passive)	"As the children listened carefully, the first soft notes were heard."	"As the children listened carefully, they heard the first soft notes."
Pronouns (Case)	"Our teacher scolded my friend and I for being late."	"Our teacher scolded my friend and *me* for being late."
Pronouns (Antecedent Agreement)	"The marketing department gives generous bonuses to their workers."	"The marketing department gives generous bonuses to *its* workers."
Pronouns (Ambiguous Antecedent)	"When the meteor hit the mountain, it exploded."	"When it hit the mountain, the meteor exploded."
Pronouns (Absent Antecedent)	"In the report they indicate that orange juice is good for you."	"The report indicates that orange juice is good for you."
Pronouns (Consistency)	"When you don't understand, one should ask for clarification."	"When you don't understand, *you* should ask for clarification."

Parallelism	"To review every week is just as important as studying every day."	"Reviewing every week is just as important as studying every day."
Parallelism (with Prepositions)	"The story takes place in Japan, not China."	"The story takes place in Japan, not *in* China."
Comparisons	"The roar of a lion is much louder than a tiger."	"The roar of a lion is much louder than *that of* a tiger."
Comparative vs. Superlative	"This question is the hardest of the two."	"This question is the *harder* of the two."
Introductory Phrases	"Walking down the pier, the seagulls were flying all around me."	"Walking down the pier, I was surrounded by flying seagulls."
Dangling Modifiers	"We had to give presentations on the Roman emperors in our class."	"In our class we had to give presentations on the Roman emperors."
Coordinating Conjunctions (Meaning)	"He finally remembered his name because he had forgotten it earlier."	"He finally remembered his name *although* he had forgotten it earlier."
Correlative Conjunctions	"Her work was not only boring, yet physically demanding as well."	"Her work was not only boring, *but also* physically demanding."
Comma Splices	"The food was very hot, it burned my tongue."	"The very hot food burned my tongue."
Redundancy	"The distant islands lay far away."	"The islands lay far away."
Diction	"The discovery affected a dramatic change in the scientists' thinking."	"The discovery *effected* a dramatic change in the scientists' thinking."
Idioms	"She preferred math over history."	"She preferred math *to* history."

Subject-Verb Agreement

A singular subject takes a singular verb, and a plural subject takes a plural verb. In the sentence "She finds some questions harder than others," the singular pronoun "she" takes the singular verb "finds." In the sentence "Many people do not manage their time well," the plural subject "many people" takes the plural verb "do."

Private Prep Tactic: To determine if a verb is singular or plural, use the "she/they" trick: place "she" and "they" in front of the verb in question and see which sounds better. For example, for the verb "studies," "she studies" sounds better than "they studies." Keep in mind that singular verbs always end in "s" while plural verbs usually do not (which is the opposite case for nouns).

Usually the subject of a sentence comes before its verb, but when the order is reversed (a structure known as inverted syntax), it is sometimes difficult to notice when a mistake is being made. For example, consider the sentence "In the desk drawer is an eraser and a few sheets of paper." To many, this might at first seem correct because it can appear that the singular verb "is" goes with the singular noun "an eraser." But the full subject is not only "an eraser," but "an eraser and a few sheets of paper," which is plural. Therefore the verb should not be "is," but "are."

Private Prep Tactic: If a sentence features inverted syntax, turn it around. For example, one could rewrite the sentence above, without changing the meaning, as: "An eraser and a few sheets of paper *are* in the desk drawer."

It is a common trick on both the ACT and SAT to place **prepositional phrases** (collections of words that begin with a preposition and, as a whole, serve the same purpose as adjectives) in between a subject and its verb. For example, in the sentence "The thick layers of grime on the ceiling and the floor has to be removed," the prepositional phrase "of grime on the ceiling and the floor" has been placed in between the subject, "layers," and the verb, "has," making it more difficult to see that the subject is the plural subject "layers," which should go with the plural verb "have" instead of the singular "has."

Private Prep Tactic: To find the subject that is governing a verb, remember to look back as far as possible instead of only looking at the words that are close to the verb. In addition, many students find it helpful to put brackets around the prepositional phrase (which begins with a preposition and usually goes all the way up to the word right before the verb) and to read what is outside the brackets. Using the example above, we would have "The thick layers [of grime on the ceiling and the floor] has to be removed," making it easier to see that "layers" cannot go with "has."

Coordinating conjunctions such as "neither," "nor," "either," "or," etc. take singular verbs when the items they are joining are singular. For example, in the sentence "Neither Mrs. James nor Mr. Brown are able to attend the meeting," both "Mrs. James" and "Mr. Brown" are singular, and therefore the plural verb "are" is incorrect and should be changed to "is." However, when both items are plural, then a plural verb is appropriate, as in the sentence "Neither ostriches nor bad ideas are able to fly."

A small minority of words, known as "**collective singulars**," which are used to describe groups, can take a plural or a singular verb, depending on the context in which they appear. For example, words such as "army," "minority," "team," and so forth take singular verbs when all the people inside them are acting as a single unit but take plural verbs when the people inside them are acting separately. For example, in the sentence "A majority often has more power than a minority," both "majority" and "minority" are being treated as single units. But in the sentence "A majority of people dream of a better life," the people are acting independently of one another (people cannot dream together), so the "majority" can take the plural verb "dream." Collective singulars do not appear often on the ACT or SAT, but it is still a good idea to become familiar with them.

Agreement and Sequence of Tenses

The tense of a verb denotes the time at which its action occurs. There are seven main tenses for English verbs, given in the chart below. Each of these can be subdivided into either simple or progressive. Students should familiarize themselves with the forms below, arranged in approximate chronological order from "most past" to "most future."

Tense	*Simple*	*Continuous*
Pluperfect	she had eaten; they had eaten	she had been eating; they had been eating
Imperfect	she used to / would eat; they used to / would eat	she would be eating; they would be eating
Past	she ate; they ate	she was eating; they were eating
Perfect	she has eaten; they have eaten	she has been eating; they have been eating
Present	she eats; they eat	she is eating; they are eating
Future Perfect	she will have eaten; they will have eaten	she will have been eating; they will have been eating
Future	she will eat; they will eat	she will be eating; they will be eating

While most students are already very familiar with the basic tenses such as past, present, and future, many do not know the rules of usage for the other tenses and should take extra care to read the explanations and rules below:

Pluperfect: This tense is used only to indicate events that occurred *before* the past. For example, in the sentence "By the time my brother called me last night, I already had eaten dinner," the verb "called" describes an action that took place in the past, and the verb "had eaten" an action that took place *before* that.

Imperfect: This tense denotes events that used to occur over a period of time at some point in the past, and can be indicated either by the words "used to" or "would," although the latter also has other meanings (see below). In the sentence "When I was younger I would go fishing with my father every weekend," it is clear that the action, fishing, took place over an extended period of time in the past.

Watch Out! The weird word "would" has three main uses in English, and to tell which is being used when, you will have to rely on context. In addition to denoting the past, the word "would" can also be used to indicate:

Hypothetical situations: events that are imagined or proposed. For example, in the sentence "I would go to the movies if you would buy my ticket," there is no guarantee of either action—the going or the buying—actually occurring. Note that this usage is similar to the subjunctive mood (see below).

Future tense from a past perspective: events that were going to occur at a later time, but prior to the present. For example, in the sentence "Twenty-five years ago my mother met the man who would become my father," both actions—the meeting and the becoming—take place in the past. But from the perspective of the mother, the second action—becoming—had not yet taken place, and was, from her point of view, the future.

Perfect: This tense is like a kind of bridge between the past and the present. It denotes either actions that began in the past and are still going on, as in the sentence "She has been reading for over an hour," in which the subject, "she," began reading in the past and is still reading now; or situations that took place in the past but may very well occur again. For example, in the sentence "I have faced many challenges," the speaker has faced challenges in the past, and there is a strong implication that she will do so again. This sense of the possibility of recurrence is what separates the perfect "I have faced," from the completed action of the past, "I faced," which simply denotes actions that are over and done with.

Watch Out! The perfect tense can be used in conjunction with the present tense, but *not* with the past. For example, the sentence "I have eaten but she still is eating," is correct, but "I have eaten but she ate" is not.

Future Perfect: This tense denotes actions that will take place in the future, but prior to some other predetermined time in the future. For example, in the sentence "By the time you graduate, you will have read many books," both actions take place in the future, but one action—the reading—takes place before the other action—graduating.

Time Indicators: Students should take care to watch out for time-words, which in and of themselves can serve to indicate what tense is appropriate for a sentence. For example, consider the sentence "For the last twenty years some of the world's leading experts worked on the problem." Here, the time words "for the last twenty years" indicate an action that was begun in the past but is still going on in the present. The past-tense verb "worked," is therefore inappropriate here, and should be replaced with the correct perfect-tense verb "have worked" or "have been working."

Verb Mood

The mood of a verb denotes the nature of the verb's action. English verbs fall into four moods, given in the table below:

Mood	Purpose	Example
Indicative	States a fact	"They study hard."
Imperative	Gives a command	"Study!"
Subjunctive	Indicates a situation is not actual	"If I were studying, I would be improving."
Infinitive	Expresses a state without action	"to study"

Most students are already familiar with the indicative, imperative, and infinitive, as these occur frequently in the English language. The subjunctive, however, bears further discussion. In the sentence above, it is clear that both actions—the studying and the improving—are not actually taking place, which is why the subjunctive verbs "were" and "would be" are used. The subjunctive mood, though relatively rare, can often appear strange to those who are unfamiliar with its forms. Students should therefore take the time to become comfortable with the examples below:

"If I were you [I am not], I would listen [though I may or may not be]."

"Had I been there [I wasn't], I would have had a great time [though I may or may not have]." (This is the same as saying, "If I had been there, I would have had a great time.")

"He need not worry about his past mistakes" (This is the same as saying, "Let him not worry about his past mistakes," and is a rather old-fashioned way of speaking; note that even though the subject, "he," is singular, there is no "s" on the end of "need.")

"God save the queen!" (This is the same as saying, "May God Save the queen!" and, like the example above, is rather old-fashioned. Again, note the lack of the "s.")

Voice

The voice of an English verb denotes whether someone or something is performing an action (active voice), or whether someone or something is receiving an action (passive voice), as shown in the table below:

Voice	Example
Active	She drives the car.
Passive	The car is driven by her.

Note that the two sentences have identical meanings and that both are correct. However, both the ACT and SAT (and many English teachers) have a strong bias against the passive voice.

 Private Prep Tactic: Whenever possible, avoid the passive voice.

 Watch Out! Inconsistency of subject is an error that often appears in conjunction with the passive voice. For example, in the sentence "Although the police searched the building carefully, nothing was found," the subject of the first clause is "the police," but the subject of the second clause is "nothing." It would be better to keep "the police" as the subject of both clauses and to change the passive voice to active: "The police searched the building but found nothing."

Noun-Number Agreement

A noun must agree in number with all other nouns to which it refers. For example, in the sentence "Gerome and his brother, Michael, were studying to become an artist," "Gerome and his brother" is plural, while "an artist" is singular, and should therefore be changed to the plural "artists" to establish agreement.

Pronouns

Students of the ACT and SAT often do not pay sufficient attention to these words because they are so common. But errors involving pronouns make up a large percentage of questions on both tests, and students should therefore be especially vigilant when dealing with these words.

Pronouns have three cases: subjective (when the pronoun is performing an action) possessive (when a pronoun owns something), and objective (when a pronoun is receiving an action). See the table below:

Subjective	Possessive	Objective
I	my / mine	me
you	your / yours	you
he	his	him
she	her / hers	her
it	its	it
we	our / ours	us
they	their / theirs	them
who	whose	whom

English prepositions always take the objective case, which is why we say, for example, "near him" instead of "near he."

 Watch Out! It used to be fairly common in spoken English for people to incorrectly use the objective case in place of the subjective case, as in the sentence "My brother and me want to go to the game." Over time, people, attempting to sound more proper, began using the subjective case—"my brother and I"—in every situation. But this is not always correct. For example, consider the sentence "The doctor told my brother and I to come back later." Because the pronoun "I" is receiving an action—"told"—it should not be in the subjective case, but the objective. Thus, "I" should be changed to "me." Whether the subjective or objective case is correct is determined solely by context. Note that the sentences "She likes Derek more than me" and "She likes Derek more than I" are both correct, but mean different things. The first means that she likes both Derek and me, but likes him more, while the second means that both she and I like Derek, but she likes him more than I do.

Private Prep Tactic: If a sentence features another person in addition to the pronoun, place brackets around that person (and the conjunction) and read what is outside the brackets. Using the sentence above, we would have "The doctor told [my brother and] I to come back later," making it easier to see that "I" should be changed to "me."

Every pronoun must follow three rules:

- o   Have a crystal-clear antecedent
- o   Agree in gender and number with that antecedent
- o   Be consistent

Recall that the antecedent is the noun (that usually comes before the pronoun) and indicates to what the pronoun is referring. For example, in the sentence "Mr. Marcus taught his students," "Mr. Marcus" is the antecedent for the pronoun "his."

Antecedent Agreement: A pronoun must agree with the gender and number of its antecedent. For example, in the sentence "Mrs. Jones asked us to visit her whenever we got the chance," the singular feminine pronoun "her" agrees with the singular feminine "Mrs. Jones."

Watch Out! In spoken English, people often use the word "they" to denote a single person who may be male or female. This is often done to avoid sounding sexist; nevertheless, it is not correct written English. On the ACT and SAT, the pronoun "they" can only refer to a plural antecedent, just as the pronoun "it" can only refer to a singular antecedent. For example, in the sentence "Every student would like to leave school on their lunch break," "their" refers to "every student," but because "every student" is singular, the plural "their" is incorrect, and the sentence should either be rewritten as "Every student would like to leave school on his or her lunch break" or as "All students would like to leave school on their lunch breaks."

Ambiguous Antecedent: Consider the sentence: "The nurse and her daughter went to her house," which features two instances of the pronoun "her." In the first instance, the antecedent is clearly the nurse. But in the second instance, it is impossible to tell whether "her" refers to the nurse or to her daughter, and the sentence is therefore incorrect; the second "her" would need to be changed to either "the latter's," "the former's," "the nurse's," or "the daughter's," etc. to establish clarity.

Absent antecedent: Also consider the sentence "On the news they said that it would rain tomorrow," in which the pronoun "they" incorrectly appears without a clear antecedent. "They" should therefore be eliminated and the sentence rewritten accordingly—as "The news forecast calls for rain tomorrow," for example.

Pronoun consistency: A pronoun must also remain consistent throughout the sentence. For example, in "If one wants to become really good at something, you need to practice every day," there is an incorrect shift from "one" to "you." The sentence should be rewritten as either "If you want to become really good at something, you need to practice every day," or "If one wants to become really good at something, one needs to practice every day" to maintain consistency.

Parallelism

Once a sentence establishes a structure, the rest of that sentence must follow that structure, unless there is a clearly indicated shift. For example, in the sentence "She is an amazing dancer, singer, and writes really well," the pattern is one of nouns—"dancer," "singer"—from which the end of the sentence "writes really well" incorrectly diverges. Instead, "writes really well" should be changed to "writer" to maintain parallelism.

Sometimes prepositions must be repeated in order to maintain parallelism. For example, the sentence "There are more bacteria in crabs than fish," is incorrect because it means that there are more bacteria in crabs than there are fish in crabs. The preposition "in" must be repeated to make it clear that "There are more bacteria in crabs than *in* fish."

Comparisons

Whenever a comparison is being made, it is important to make sure that it is between two things of the same category. For example, in the sentence "Some consider the art of the Egyptians more valuable than the Romans," a product ("art") is being compared to a people ("Romans"). Instead, we should be comparing art to art, as in "Some consider the art of the Egyptians more valuable than the Romans'," [Note the apostrophe after the "s"], or, more commonly, "Some consider the art of the Egyptians more valuable than *that of* the Romans."

Most adjectives have three forms: the positive, the comparative, and the superlative, which are used, respectively, to describe one, two, or three or more nouns. For example, "bad" is the positive form, "worse" the comparative, and "worst" the superlative. When adjectives are being used to compare two or more nouns, it is important to see whether the comparative or superlative form is appropriate. Consider the sentence "Of the two brothers, Tom is the oldest." This is incorrect because the superlative form, "oldest," must refer to three or more nouns, and this sentence only features two. The correct sentence would therefore be "Of the two brothers, Tom is the *older*."

Introductory Phrases and Dangling Modifiers

An introductory phrase comes at the beginning of a sentence, before the subject, and must describe that subject. For example, in the sentence "working hard every day, she made progress," "working hard every day" comes before and describes the subject, "she." Whenever a sentence includes an introductory phrase, it is essential to determine whether the phrase is describing the subject, as it should, or incorrectly referring to something else. For example, in the sentence "strolling down the road, many beautiful houses appeared before us," the introductory phrase, "strolling down the road," is describing the subject, "many beautiful houses," which makes no sense because houses cannot stroll. A correct alternative would be "strolling down the road, we saw many beautiful houses," where the same introductory phrase would now correctly refer to "we."

Dangling modifiers are similar to incorrect introductory phrases, except that they come at the end of a sentence instead of at the beginning. For example, in the sentence "at his house, Mr. Smith served a traditional Thanksgiving turkey dressed in Pilgrims' clothes," because there is no separation between the noun, "turkey" and the participial adjective "dressed," the two go together. In other words, it is the turkey, not Mr. Smith, that is dressed in Pilgrims' clothes. In order to correct this, we would simply place a comma between "turkey" and "dressed" to indicate that the two do not go together: "at his house, Mr. Smith served a traditional Thanksgiving turkey, dressed in Pilgrims' clothes." Since it is now clear that "dressed" does not refer to the turkey, it must refer back to the next closest noun, Mr. Smith. Alternatively, we could place the descriptive phrase closer to the noun it modifies, as in "At his house, Mr. Smith, dressed in Pilgrims' clothes, served a traditional Thanksgiving turkey."

Coordinating and Correlative Conjunctions

Coordinating conjunctions, such as "and," "although," "because," "but," "yet," "or," "nor," "so," and "for" express the logical relationship between different items or ideas. When dealing with these conjunctions, it is important to determine whether they are being used appropriately in their given context. For example, in the sentence "Julie was sincere, generous, and kind, but everybody liked her," the coordinating conjunction, "but," which serves to illustrate a contrast, is being used to connect two ideas that agree with each other. A correct alternative would be "Julie was sincere, generous, and kind, *so* everybody liked her," in which the conjunction "so," which serves to illustrate cause or agreement, is doing so.

 Watch Out! Although the word "for" is often used as a preposition, as in "The teacher brought handouts for her students," it can also be used as a coordinating conjunction that expresses cause. For example, in the sentence "He didn't know which way to go, for there were many different roads," "for" serves as a coordinating conjunction that means "because."

Conjunctions are sometimes used unnecessarily to separate two ideas that are actually one and the same. For example, in the sentence "Edward has a problem, and it is very bad," the conjunction "and," which serves to introduce a new piece of information, is instead being used to elaborate on what has already been stated. It would be simpler, and better, to eliminate the unnecessary conjunction, as in "Edward has a very bad problem."

 Private Prep Tactic: Whenever you encounter a pronoun, ask yourself if it, and/or the clause it governs, is really necessary. For example, in the sentence above, the pronoun "it" isn't needed. Watching out for unnecessary pronouns can help alert you to the presence of errors.

Correlative Conjunctions are pairs of conjunctions, such as "either...or," "neither...nor," "not only...but also," "so...that," and "as...as" that work together to express the logical relationship between different items or ideas, and, very often, are inseparable in the sense that one cannot appear without the other. For example, in the sentence "Angela's backpack was so heavy and she had to stop several times," the correlative conjunction "so" is incorrectly paired with the conjunction "and" instead of "that," as in the correct sentence "Angela's backpack was so heavy *that* she had to stop several times."

 Watch Out! The conjunctions "either...or" and "neither...nor" take verbs that agree with the number of things that they are joining: singular verbs for singular items, plural verbs for plural items. For example, in the sentence "neither Henry nor Harriet are coming to the party," each noun, "Henry" and "Harriet" is singular, and therefore the plural verb, "are" is incorrect. The correct sentence would be "neither Henry nor Harriet *is* coming to the party."

Comma Splices, Semicolons, and Colons

Although the comma has more uses than any other punctuation mark, it can't do everything. For example, a comma cannot separate two independent clauses; when it does so, it produces an error known as a comma splice. However, a comma *and a conjunction* can be used together to separate two independent clauses. For example, the sentence "we really wanted to sit down, there were so few seats," features a comma splice, which could be fixed by adding a conjunction such as "but": "we really wanted to sit down, but there were so few seats."

On the SAT and ACT, a semicolon (;) serves only to separate two independent clauses whose meanings are closely related, usually in one of three ways: 1) cause and effect, 2) contrast, and 3) explanation or elaboration. For example, in the sentence "The car broke down; we had to walk home," the first clause expresses a cause, and the second one an effect. In "I loved the movie; she hated it," the semicolon indicates that there is contrast between the two clauses. In the sentence "Her brother was very upset; maybe she shouldn't have hung up on him," the second clause elaborates on the first. In the sentence "although James had often thought of traveling; he never found the time," the semicolon is incorrect, because "although James had often thought of traveling" is a dependent—not independent—clause; the semicolon should therefore be changed to a comma.

Colons *can* separate two independent clauses, but do not have to. One of the most common uses of a colon is to introduce a statement or list, as in the sentence "At the store he bought four things: milk, bread, butter, and eggs." However, colons can also serve to separate two independent clauses when the first clause makes a claim for which the second clause provides support, as in the sentence "He was a very wealthy man: he owned over twenty highly successful companies." In either case, the clause before a colon *must* be independent.

 Private Prep Tactic: Whenever given the choice between separating two independent clauses or joining them, try the latter. Consider the incorrect sentence "the baseball players were having a hard time, some of their best players were injured," which features a comma splice. There are three ways to correct this error:

1. Separate the two independent clauses with proper punctuation: "The baseball players were having a hard time; some of their best players were injured"
2. Make one of the independent clauses into a dependent clause and join the two together: "The baseball players were having a hard time because some of their best players were injured." In this case, the insertion of the word "because" into the second clause makes it into a dependent clause, allowing it to be joined together with the independent clause that precedes it.
3. Make the second clause dependent and change its position in the sentence: "Because some of their best players were injured, the baseball players were having a hard time."

All three methods are correct, but it is more common, especially on the SAT and ACT, to join two clauses, as in examples 2 and 3 above, than to separate them.

Redundancy

Redundancy is the unnecessary repetition of ideas. It can sometimes be difficult to notice redundancy because it is not, technically speaking, a grammatical error, but a problem with meaning. For example, in the sentence "every year the scientists returned to the site to measure the annual rainfall," the words "every year" and "annual" mean the same thing; either "every year" or "annual" should therefore be eliminated. Note that redundancy is very common on the ACT, and is becoming increasingly popular on the SAT.

Diction and Idioms

Diction refers not to the grammatical role of words, but to their traditional usage and/or meaning. For example, in the sentence "Her enemies tried to scatter a bad rumor about her," the verb "scatter" is operating in a grammatically correct way, but is not in line with traditional usage. One does not scatter a rumor; one *spreads* a rumor. Proper diction is far too complex and arbitrary to be defined by any predetermined system of rules, so diction errors can be hard to spot. Fortunately, these errors are fairly rare on the ACT and SAT.

Idioms are set expressions that, like proper diction, are defined by traditional usage. For example, in the sentence "many of the spectators themselves had a powerful preoccupation for cars," there is no rule that explains why the preposition "for" is incorrect—it just is. One does not have a preoccupation for something, but a preoccupation *with* something. Fortunately, these kinds of errors are also fairly rare.

Homophones

Homophones are words that sound alike but have different meanings. Because people often rely on how something sounds to help them determine whether it is correct, homophones can pose a special problem. Students should therefore review the meanings of the following words (and non-words):

there: refers to a place, as in "I'll meet you over there."

they're: a contraction of "they are," as in "They're making too much noise."

their: the possessive form of "they," as in, "They need to take their car to the shop."

who's: a contraction of "who is," as in "Look who's coming to dinner."

whose: the possessive form of "who," as in "Whose motorcycle is this?"

it's: a contraction of "it is," as in "It's hot in here."

its: the possessive form of "it," as in "A chain is only as strong as its weakest link."

its': this is NOT a word, though it may appear in some answer choices on the ACT.

"Then" vs. "Than":
Though these two words sound alike, they have totally different meanings. "Then" refers to a time or a next step, as in "back then life seemed simpler," or "then mix in the sugar." "Than" refers to a comparison, as in "She is smarter than I."

"Could've," "Should've," "Would've":
The words "could've," "should've," and "would've" are contractions, respectively, of "could have," "would have," and "should have," and are grammatically correct. Students should be aware, however, that the phrases "could of," "should of," and "would of," which sound similar, simply do not exist; they are INCORRECT.

Apostrophes
These punctuation marks serve to indicate either an omission or possession; context often determines which. By way of example, we will be using the words "boy" and "men."

"boy's": the "'s" indicates either singular possessive, as in "they boy's clothes," or the contraction for "boy is," as in "The boy's nice." Context will determine which.

"boys'": the "s'" indicates plural possessive, as in "the boys' houses." Note that the "s'" ending is used for words whose plurals end in "s." For words whose plurals do not end in "s," see the description of "men's" below.

"men's": the plural possessive, as in "the men's qualifications." Note that because the plural "men" does not end in s, we add an "s'" to make it plural.

"mens'"/ "mens's": these are NOT words, though they may appear in answer choices on the ACT.

 Watch Out! An apostrophe is often required to indicate the connection between two nouns. For example, the phrase "the countries capitals" is incorrect; it should be "the countries' capitals." Remember—no apostrophe, no connection

Sentence Diagramming: A Condensed Grammar and Sentence Structure Guide

The Independent Clause (Basic Sentence)

To write a complete sentence, all we need is an independent clause. That's one subject *plus one* main verb. *The subject tells us "what/who" and the main verb tells us "does what."*

Example: The dog runs. = (The dog) + runs. Independent clause ✓

Subjects can be pronouns and other words that refer to nouns. The following are complete sentences and do not have to make sense out of context.

Many run.

They run.

Some run.

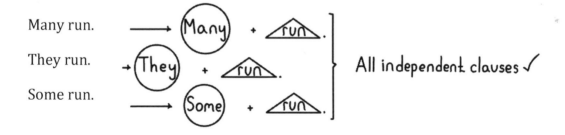

All independent clauses ✓

Subjects can also be gerunds. The following are complete sentences.

Walking is fun.

Running hurts.

Yes, the verb "to be" is still a verb. The following are complete sentences.

Dogs are happy.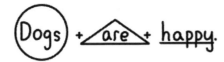

Many are friends.

Some were puppies.

To any basic sentence, we can add all sorts of adjectives and adverbs. You only need to consider punctuation when listing multiple adjectives or adverbs in a row. (On the SAT you can be confident using commas to separate lists of three or more adjectives or adverbs. When it comes to lists of 2, commas are only sometimes necessary.)

The fluffy and overweight dog runs slowly.

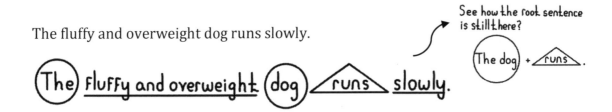

The tiny, skinny, incorrigible dog ran quickly and with ease.

When you are thinking about how a sentence is constructed, you can think of <u>adjectives</u> and <u>adverbs</u> as integral parts, respectively, of the subject phrase or the verb phrase of the sentence. You can also think of articles (words like "a") as part of the subject phrase and the verb's objects (in the phrases "went home" and "is happy", home and happy are the verb's objects) as part of the verb phrase. An object is simply the person or thing the verb acts upon. For example, in the first example sentence, the verb's object is "the ball", which becomes part of the verb phrase.

The dog caught the ball.

The fluffy dog runs slowly.

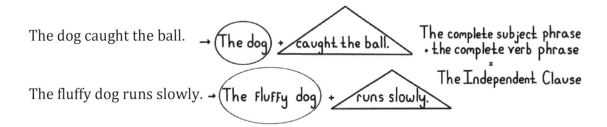

The tiny, skinny, incorrigible dog was running quickly and with ease.

Adding a Prepositional Phrase

We can add a <u>prepositional phrase</u> to the root sentence to give direction/place/time. Prepositional Phrases can be attached to the front, middle, or the end of any independent clause.

The fluffy dogs run around the lake.

(The fluffy dogs) · ◁run▷ · <u>around the lake</u>.

Around the lake, some fluffy dogs are running.

The dogs in the lake are swimming.

Prepositional phrases can be as long as you want, and you can use as many as you want in a single sentence.

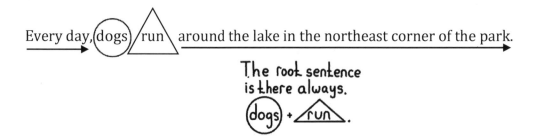

Every day, (dogs) /run\ around the lake in the northeast corner of the park.

The root sentence
is there always.
(dogs) + /run\ .

Tiny, scrawny dogs run around the enormous man-made lake in the northeast corner of Central Park in New York every morning.

Adding Restrictive and Non-Restrictive Clauses and Phrases

Now we can insert additional phrases and clauses into the beginning, middle, or end of the root sentence.

We could add a | dependent clause | *to the beginning of an independent clause, separating it with a comma:*

Unaware of world events, dogs run blissfully through the park.

= | Unaware of world events |, + (dogs) + /run blissfuly\ + through the park.

Or after an independent clause with no comma:

In the park, dogs run without any awareness of world events.

= In the park, + (dogs) + /run\ + | without any awareness of world events. |

Or we could insert a clause into the middle of the basic sentence.

Example 1: Dogs, unaware of world events, run blissfully through the park.

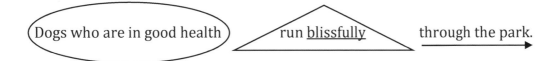

Example 2: Dogs who are in good health run blissfully through the park.

Private Prep Tactic

In the examples above, notice you have two options for punctuation: bookend the information with commas/dashes, or don't. The rule is simple: if the information defines the subject of the sentence, it is **essential** and becomes part of the sentence without punctuation. If the information does not define the subject of the sentence, it is **non-essential** and should be separated from the sentence with commas. In example 1 above, all/any dogs run blissfully through the park. The information that they are "unaware of world events" does not change the subject—dogs—and is therefore **non-essential.** We separate with commas (or dashes). In example 2, only dogs "who are in good health" run through the park. Because the information—"who are in good health"—defines the subject of the sentence (it specifies that we are talking only about dogs who are in good health), it is **essential,** and there are consequently no commas.

When you are thinking about how sentences are constructed, you can think of essential clauses as part of the subject of the sentence:

Remember your participial phrases. These are phrases introduced by present or past participles (those words ending in -ing or -ed), which function as adjectives in the sentence.)

Many, running through the park at night, are frightened.

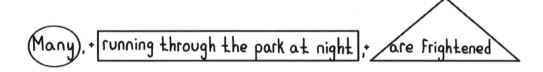

The dogs running through my back yard seem frightened.

Golden retrievers, considered old fashioned by some, are, in fact, the hippest breed.

Phrases/clauses inserted into the basic sentence can be as long or short as you want, and you can use as many as you want.

Terriers, lean and crafty, hunt squirrels.

My own dog, Fred—whose piercing white eyes suggest a near descent from wolves and frighten people and other dogs alike—is, in actuality, a loving animal and member of our family.

Her dog's leash, which extends impractically to 100 feet, gets tangled in many bushes.

Originally bred for aquatic retrieval, the black lab, America's most popular breed, loves the water.

Some—chihuahuas and pugs among them—fear the ocean.

Transitions

Sometimes you want to transition within a sentence. Transitions can be added to the beginning, middle, or end of basic sentences, or they can start new sentences.

However, my dog is not very fast.

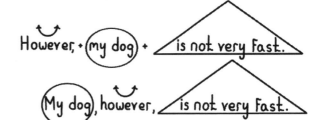

My dog, however, is not very fast.

My dog is not very fast, however.

My dog runs; however, he is not very fast.

Private Prep Tactic

Notice how lonely the transition is. It is separated from the rest of the sentence by punctuation on both sides. It's an interruption, and it needs to be treated as such.

Dogs, on the other hand, are quite intelligent.

Meanwhile, my dog—a black lab—refuses to get out of the water.

He eats, for example, tacos and spaghetti.

Joining additional independent clauses

The root sentence is an independent clause: a subject plus a main verb. As we've seen, the root sentence often includes additional information such as prepositional phrases and additional clauses. But remember: there is only one main subject. If we want to add another main subject, we can do that.

We can join multiple independent clauses together in various ways. Following are some of the most common found on the SAT.

We could join two independent clauses together with for/and/nor/but/or/yet/so plus a comma:

One dog runs, and another dog walks.

Or we could use a semicolon:

Her dog runs; she walks.

Or we could use a semicolon plus a transition:

My dog will run; however, he prefers to walk.

Putting it all together

With multiple independent clauses joined together and additional information embedded within each clause, sentences can get long and complex. But if you can see the underlying structure, all the joints make sense.

Some trainers believe city dogs are fundamentally different from country dogs. However, the psychology of canines, an ancient species, is always rooted in the earth; yes, some—chihuahuas and pugs among them—may fear the ocean, but all breeds, their senses attuned to nature's harvest, will enjoy time spent on Lake Winnipesaukee in the fall.

Try to put it all together!

CHAPTER 2: MATH

PATHWAYS INTRODUCTION

Problem solving in Math can take many forms. Everybody's brain works differently, so some people are more comfortable solving problems one way, while other people are more comfortable solving in a different way. Many (if not most!) math problems offer the opportunity to solve in multiple ways.

That said, there are still some important steps everyone should take before they jump into problem solving. Be sure to always follow the first 3 steps listed below before jumping into a forwards or backwards approach.

1. Identify the goal of the problem and circle/underline it.
2. Underline/circle information that is given in the problem.
3. Categorize the type of math that the question is asking for.
   - Write down any formulas that you think might be relevant.

There are two primary ways to problem solve:

Attempt the **FORWARDS** breakdown

- What is given in the problem?
  - Rewrite given information if the text is difficult to interpret. Attempt to translate word problems into equations or mathematical operations.
  - Does any of the given information match with any formulas you wrote down?
  - Can anything be done to the information to manipulate it?
    - Once you manipulate, has the information begun to look like it fits into a known pattern or formula?
- Is there any information you haven't used yet?

Attempt the **BACKWARDS** breakdown

- Do any of the answer choices make absolutely no sense? Eliminate them!
  - Do you see negative values when you know the number should be positive?
  - Do you see numbers that are way too small or large given the problem?
- Is it possible to check the answer choices using relevant formulas?
- Is there an image or picture that you can use to estimate?
- Can you plug your own numbers into the problem?

Did you get stuck using either approach? Remember that SWITCHING GEARS to the other approach can be a useful way to reset your perspective to see what you are missing.

Did you work through the problem confidently and get a number that isn't there?

- Go back to the goal of problem. Be sure you didn't solve for a different value than the one being asked for.
- Did you consider the units that the problem used?
    - Be sure to adjust all units to match the answers before you start plugging things into your calculator.
- Are the answers in the form of an expression rather than decimal form?
- Did you plug one large expression into your calculator?
    - Plug in one operation at a time, write down your calculator output, and feed it back into the next operation.
    - Double check to see if you used parentheses appropriately.
- Did you distribute the negatives correctly?

PATHWAY WALKTHROUGH

1. Which of the following is a solution to the equation
   $x^2 - 100x = 0$?
   A. 200
   B. 100
   C. 50
   D. 10
   E. -10

Forwards

$$x(x-100) = 0$$

$x = 0$	$x - 100 = 0$
	$+100 \quad +100$
	$x = 100$

Backwards

-Use your calculator & plug-in answer choices
-Always start in the middle, so you know if you need a larger or smaller answer.

$(50)^2 - 100(50) = 0$

$2500 - 5000 = -2500$ (NOT 0)

*answer is negative, so we need to plug in a larger value to get to 0.

$(100)^2 - 100(100) = 0$

$10,000 - 10,000 = 0 \checkmark$

2. If x and y are both negative integers, which of the
   following must be true?
   A. $x - y > 0$
   B. $\sqrt{xy} > 0$
   C. $x^2 y > 0$
   D. $|x| + y > 0$
   E. $xy < 0$

Forwards

Backwards

Let's plug in numbers to test the answer choices.

Say x = -3 and y = -4

A. (-3)-(-4) = -3+4 = 1

   1>0, so A. can work, but we don't know that it
   MUST work.

B. $\sqrt{(-3)(-4)}$ = $\sqrt{12}$

   $\sqrt{12}$ >0, so B. works too.

C. $(-3)^2(-4)$ = -36

   -36<0, so eliminate C.

D. |-3| +(-4) = -1

   -1<0, so eliminate D.

E. (-3)(-4) =12 12>0, so eliminate E.

Now only A and B are left. Let's try other values of
x and y to see if we can disprove one of the choices.

Say x = -5 and y = -3

A. (-5)-(-3)= -2

   -2<0, so eliminate A.

We are left with $\boxed{B.}$ as the only possible answer.

When a question has answer choices that are exclusively variables, working backwards by
plugging in numbers is almost always the best route.

3. When x = 5, which of the following is equivalent to

$$\frac{x^2 - x - 6}{x - 3} \ ?$$

    A. -2

    B. 0

    C. 4

    D. 7

    E. 15

Forwards

$$\frac{x^2-x-6}{x-3} \qquad x=5$$

$$\frac{(5)^2-(5)-6}{(5)-3} = \frac{25-5-6}{5-3} = \frac{14}{2} = 7 \ \boxed{D} \ \checkmark$$

Backwards

$$\frac{x^2-x-6}{x-3} = \frac{\cancel{(x-3)}(x+2)}{\cancel{x-3}}$$

$$= x+2$$

C. $x+2=4$

    $-2 \ -2$

    $x = 2 \leftarrow$ too small

D. $x+2=7$

    $-2 \ -2$

    $x = 5 \ \boxed{D} \checkmark$

4. Craig's Carpets is installing new carpet in a customer's living room. The installer notes that the area of the rectangular room is 120 square meters and that the perimeter is 46 meters. The installer lost the paperwork with the room's dimensions. What are the dimensions of the room, in meters?

A. 6 by 20
B. 20 by 13
C. 12 by 10
D. 15 by 8
E. 16 by 7

Forwards

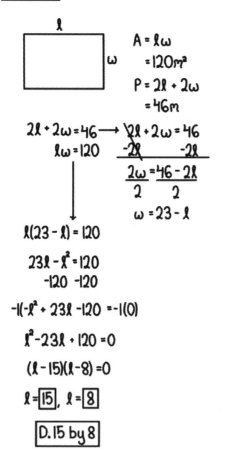

$$A = \ell w$$
$$= 120 m^2$$
$$P = 2\ell + 2w$$
$$= 46 m$$

$$2\ell + 2w = 46 \longrightarrow 2\ell + 2w = 46$$
$$\ell w = 120 \qquad -2\ell \qquad -2\ell$$
$$\frac{2w = 46 - 2\ell}{2}$$
$$w = 23 - \ell$$

$$\ell(23 - \ell) = 120$$

$$23\ell - \ell^2 = 120$$
$$-120 \quad -120$$

$$-1(-\ell^2 + 23\ell - 120 = -1(0)$$

$$\ell^2 - 23\ell + 120 = 0$$

$$(\ell - 15)(\ell - 8) = 0$$

$$\ell = \boxed{15}, \ \ell = \boxed{8}$$

$$\boxed{\text{D. 15 by 8}}$$

Backwards

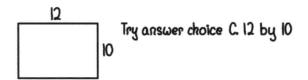

Try answer choice C. 12 by 10

$$A = \ell w = 12 \cdot 10 = \boxed{120} \checkmark$$
that works!

$$P = 2\ell + 2w$$
$$= 2(12) + 2(10) = 24 + 20 = \boxed{44} \times$$
that does not...

- -

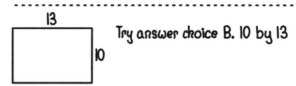

Try answer choice B. 10 by 13

$$A = \ell w = 10 \cdot 13 = \boxed{130} \times$$
nope...

- -

Try answer choice D. 15 by 8

$$A = \ell w = 15 \cdot 8 = \boxed{120} \checkmark$$
correct

$$P = 2(15) + 2(8) = 30 + 16 = \boxed{46} \checkmark$$
yes!

$$\boxed{\text{D. 15 by 8}}$$

5. Joe found $13.22 in pennies, nickels, dimes, and quarters while walking home from school one week. When he deposited this money in the bank, he noticed that he had twice as many dimes as pennies, 1 more dime than nickels, and 1 fewer quarter than nickels. How many quarters did Joe find that week?

   A. 18
   B. 19
   C. 28
   D. 29
   E. 32

Forwards

① Setup equations that relate the information given.

$$13.22 = 0.01(P) + 0.1(D) + 0.05(N) + 0.25(Q)$$

$D = 2P \rightarrow$ people often flip this, so be careful!
$N + 1 = D$
$N - 1 = Q$

② Express the quantity of each coin in terms of quarters.

$N - 1 = Q \rightarrow Q + 1 = N$ ✓

$N + 1 = D \rightarrow Q + 1 + 1 = D \rightarrow Q + 2 = D$ ✓

$D = 2P \rightarrow Q + 2 = 2P \rightarrow \dfrac{Q + 2}{2} = P$ ✓

③ Plug these 3 expressions into the first equation, and solve for Q.

$$13.22 = 0.01\left(\frac{Q+2}{2}\right) + 0.05(Q+1) + 0.1(Q+2) + 0.25(Q)$$

↓ ↓ ↓ ↓ ↓

Many steps later, assuming that nothing goes wrong in the manipulation, you will obtain $\boxed{Q = 32}$

Backwards

① Start with the middle answer choice and work backwards.

→ If $Q = 28$ then we have 29 nickels, 30 dimes, and 15 pennies.

$$(28)0.25 + (29)0.05 + (30)0.1 + (15)0.01 = ?$$
$$7 + 1.45 + 3 + 0.15 = 11.6$$

That's not enough money, so we should try 29 quarters.

→ If $Q = 29$, then we have 30 nickels, 31 dimes... and 15.5 pennies?

↓

THAT'S IMPOSSIBLE!

→ The correct answer must be $\boxed{\text{32 quarters.}}$

6. Square ABED has a side length of 12. Point C is the midpoint of AB. What is the length of CE?

    A. 9

    B. 12

    C. $6\sqrt{5}$

    D. $\sqrt{258}$

    E. 18

<u>Forwards</u>

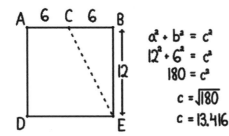

$$a^2 + b^2 = c^2$$
$$12^2 + 6^2 = c^2$$
$$180 = c^2$$
$$c = \sqrt{180}$$
$$c = 13.416$$

→At this point we could shift gears to backwards solving and convert the answers to decimals

. . .

or we could simplify:

$\sqrt{180} = \sqrt{3}\,\sqrt{3}\,\sqrt{2}\,\sqrt{2}\,\sqrt{5}$

$\boxed{= 6\sqrt{5}}$

<u>Backwards</u>

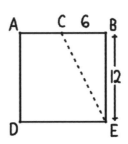

→CE, the hypotenuse, must be longer than 12, the leg.

    Eliminate F and G.

→The sum of legs BC and BE must be greater than CE. 6 + 12 = 18

    Eliminate K.

→H. $6\sqrt{5} = 13.46$

    J. $\sqrt{258} = 16.062$

If we eyeball it (or measure with the page), CE is slightly longer than BE, so H. is the better choice.

Sometimes it makes sense to set the problem up as if to solve forwards. From that point, you can continue the forward route or switch gears and backsolve.

7. In the circle with center Z shown below, the length of radius ZW is 7 cm, the length of WX is 2 cm, and WX is perpendicular to radius YZ at X. When angle WZY is measured in degrees, which of the following expressions represents the length, in centimeters, of minor arc $\widehat{WY}$?

A. $\dfrac{7\pi}{180}\left(\sin^{-1}\left(\dfrac{2}{7}\right)\right)$

B. $\dfrac{14\pi}{180}\left(\cos^{-1}\left(\dfrac{2}{7}\right)\right)$

C. $\dfrac{14\pi}{180}\left(\sin^{-1}\left(\dfrac{2}{7}\right)\right)$

D. $\dfrac{14\pi}{180}\left(\tan^{-1}\left(\dfrac{2}{7}\right)\right)$

E. $\dfrac{7\pi}{180}\left(\cos^{-1}\left(\dfrac{2}{7}\right)\right)$

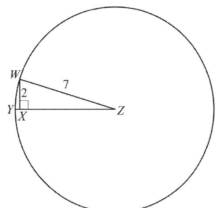

Forwards

① $\dfrac{\theta}{360} = \dfrac{\text{arc length}}{2\pi r}$

We have enough information to solve for our angle θ, so that is where we will start.

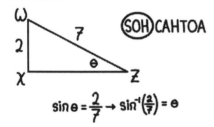

(SOH)CAHTOA

$\sin\theta = \dfrac{2}{7} \rightarrow \sin^{-1}\left(\dfrac{2}{7}\right) = \theta$

② Now plug θ and the radius into the formula for arc length.

$\dfrac{\sin^{-1}\left(\frac{2}{7}\right)}{360} = \dfrac{\text{arc length}}{14\pi}$

$\dfrac{14\pi\sin^{-1}\left(\frac{2}{7}\right)}{360} = \boxed{\dfrac{7\pi\sin^{-1}\left(\frac{2}{7}\right)}{180}}$

Backwards

① By looking at the image, we can estimate that the arc length should be a bit longer than WX, so it should be a bit larger than 2.

② Plug the answer choices into the calculator to see which ones give a number slightly larger than 2.

A. 2.02 ✓

B. 17.93 ✗

C. 4.06 ✗

D. 3.90 ✗

E. 8.97 ✗

PRACTICE QUESTIONS

8. Which of the following is a solution to the equation
   $x^2 - 24x = 0$?
   A. -48
   B. -24
   C. 12
   D. 24
   E. 48

9. If $12x = -8(5 - x)$, then $x = ?$
   A. -10
   B. -2
   C. 1/10
   D. 2
   E. 10

10. In the complex numbers, where $i^2 = -1$,
$$\frac{1}{1-i} \cdot \frac{1+i}{1+i} = ?$$

   A. $1 - i$
   B. $1 + i$
   C. i
   D. $\dfrac{-(1+i)}{2}$
   E. $\dfrac{1+i}{2}$

11. If x and y are integers, x is negative, and $x^3y^5 > 0$,
    which of the following must be true?
    A. $y > 0$
    B. $x - y > 0$
    C. $xy > 0$
    D. $y - x > 0$
    E. $xy^2 > 0$

12. What are the possible values of b if $a^3b^2 = 72$ when a
    and b are both integers?
    A. 3
    B. -6, 6
    C. 1, 6
    D. -3, 3
    E. 6

13. Given that y is negative, x is positive, and $\frac{x+y}{x} = a$, which of the following must be true for a?
    A. $|a| < 1$
    B. $a > 0$
    C. $a > -1$
    D. $a > 1$
    E. $a < 1$

14. When y = -3, which of the following is equivalent to
$$\frac{y + 2}{y^2 - 5y - 14} =?$$
    A. -1/8
    B. -1/10
    C. 1/20
    D. 1/10
    E. 1/8

15. If $f(x) = x^2 - x - 20$ and $f(x) = -8$, which of the following are possible values of x?
    A. 0 only
    B. -3 only
    C. 4 only
    D. -3 and 4
    E. -3, 0, and 4

16. In the equation $\frac{x^2+3x}{x+3} = 5$, x must be equal to which of the following?
    A. -5
    B. -1
    C. 3
    D. 5
    E. 10

17. The area of a new rectangular playground will be 210 ft^2. The playground will have a log border that has a total length of 74 ft. What are the dimensions of the playground, in feet?
    A. 7 by 30
    B. 8 by 29
    C. 10 by 21
    D. 14 by 15
    E. 16 by 21

18. The length of a rectangle is 3 more than twice the width. The area of the rectangle is 230 square units. Which of the following could be the width, in units, of the rectangle?

A. 8
B. 10
C. 13
D. 23
E. 32

19. A pool holds 880,000 liters of water and is 10 meters long. Which of the following could be the length and height of the pool, respectively?
(Note: 1000 L = 1 cubic meter)

A. 22 m,. 4 m
B. 20 m, 5 m
C. 18 m, 6 m
D. 17 m, 5 m
E. 16 m, 6 m

20. Jackpot! The next week, Joe found $120.95 while walking home from school. When he deposited the money in the bank, he noticed that he had three times as many quarters as pennies, 1 more quarter than nickels, and 1 fewer nickel than dimes. How many nickels did Joe find that week?

A. 50
B. 100
C. 299
D. 300
E. 301

21. Tickets for a high school's theater production cost $5 each when bought in advance and $10 each when bought at the door. The theater group's goal is at least $2,000 in ticket sales for opening night. The theater sold 140 opening-night tickets in advance. What is the minimum number of tickets they need to sell at the door on opening night to make their goal?

A. 50
B. 130
C. 140
D. 150
E. 200

22. After all of the shows, the high school recorded their final ticket sales. Tickets purchased in advance cost $8 and tickets purchased at the door cost $12. The table below shows the tickets sold per night both in advance and at the door.

	Friday	Saturday
Advance	85	123
At the Door	152	101

For which night did the school earn more in ticket sales, and by how much?

A. Friday, by $308
B. Friday, by $300
C. Saturday, by $120
D. Saturday, by $300
E. Saturday, by $308

23. Rectangle $ABCD$ has a side length of 20 and a width of 15. What is the distance of $\overline{AC}$?

A. $10\sqrt{5}$
B. $15\sqrt{2}$
C. $45/2$
D. 25
E. 35

Figure: rectangle ABCD with vertices A (top-left), B (top-right), D (bottom-left), C (bottom-right).

24. What is the height of the equilateral triangle that has a side length of 4?

A. 2
B. $2\sqrt{2}$
C. 3
D. $2\sqrt{3}$
E. 4

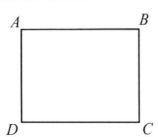

25. In right triangle △ABC, sin(B) = 3/5. Which of the following expressions is equal to cos(B)?

A. 2/5
B. 1/2
C. 1
D. 5/3
E. 4/5

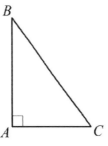

26. In the circle with center A, radius $\overline{AB}$ measures 4 inches. △ABC is a right isosceles triangle. What expression is equal to the measure of minor arc $\overset{\frown}{BD}$?

A. $\dfrac{(4\pi)(30)}{360}$

B. $\dfrac{(4\pi)(45)}{360}$

C. $\dfrac{(4\pi)(60)}{360}$

D. $\dfrac{(8\pi)(45)}{360}$

E. $\dfrac{(8\pi)(90)}{360}$

27. Which expression gives the area of the trapezoid shown below?

A. $\dfrac{(10)(15)}{2}$

B. $\dfrac{(10)(30)}{2}$

C. $\dfrac{(10)(18)}{2}$

D. $\dfrac{(10)(12)}{2}$

E. $\dfrac{(10)(12)(18)}{2}$

28. At the start of a play, the quarterback is at point Q. The receiver is at point R_1, 18 yards from the quarterback. The receiver catches a pass at point R_2, 55 yards away from the quarterback. If the quarterback pivoted 35° while tracking the receiver's run, how far did the receiver run from the start of play to when the pass was caught?

(Note: the law of cosines states that for any triangle with vertices A, B, and C, and the sides opposite those vertices with lengths a, b, and c, respectively, $c^2 = a^2 + b^2 - 2ab \cos C$)

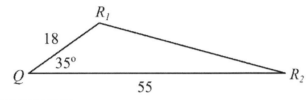

A. $\sqrt{55^2 - 18^2}$

B. $\sqrt{55^2 + 18^2 - 2(55)(18)\cos 35}$

C. $\sqrt{55^2 + 18^2 + 2(55)(18)\cos 35}$

D. $\sqrt{55^2 + 18^2 - 2(55)(18)\cos 145}$

E. $\sqrt{55^2 + 18^2 + 2(55)(18)\cos 145}$

EXPLANATION ANSWERS

1. B
2. B
3. D
4. D
5. E
6. C
7. A

PRACTICE QUESTION ANSWERS

8. D
9. A
10. E
11. C
12. D
13. A
14. B
15. D
16. D
17. A
18. B
19. A
20. C
21. B
22. A
23. D
24. D
25. E
26. D
27. B
28. B

Private Prep "Need to Know" Math Facts

EXPONENT RULES

$$x^a \cdot x^b = x^{a+b} \qquad x^{-n} = \frac{1}{x^n}$$

$$\frac{x^a}{x^b} = x^{a-b} \qquad x^{\frac{a}{b}} = \sqrt[b]{x^a}$$

$$(x^a)^b = x^{ab} \qquad x^0 = 1$$

$$\qquad\qquad\qquad x^1 = x$$

$$2^2 = 4 \qquad\qquad 3^2 = 9$$

$$2^3 = 8 \qquad\qquad 3^3 = 27$$

$$2^4 = 16 \qquad\qquad 3^4 = 81$$

IMPORTANT NUMBER FACTS

Integer: "whole" numbers — positive, negative, or zero.

Zero: neither positive nor negative. Zero is even.

Primes: 1 isn't prime. 2 is the only even prime.

PYTHAGOREAN THEOREM
$$a^2 + b^2 = c^2$$

Triples
3—4—5
6—8—10
5—12—13
8—15—17
7—24—25

TRANSLATION

Is	means	**equals**
Of	means	**multiply**
Per	means	**divide**
Cent	means	**100**
Difference	means	**subtract**
What or	means	x
A Number		

SPECIAL RIGHT TRIANGLES

$$30° - 60° - 90° \qquad 45° - 45° - 90°$$

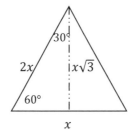 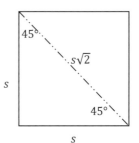

CIRCLE

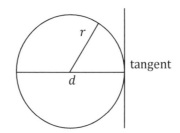

$$A = \pi r^2$$

$$C = 2\pi r = \pi d$$

RECTANGLE

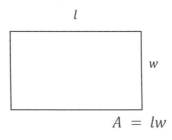

$$A = lw$$

$$P = 2l + 2w$$

Equation of a Line

slope-intercept: $y = mx + b$

slope: $m = \dfrac{rise}{run} = \dfrac{\Delta y}{\Delta x} = \dfrac{y_2 - y_1}{x_2 - x_1}$

y-intercept: b

x-intercept: $-b/m$

point-slope: $(y - y_1) = m(x - x_1)$

Transformations

$y = f(x) + b$: up b

$y = f(x) - b$: down b

$y = f(x + b)$: left b

$y = f(x - b)$: right b

Parabolas

$y = a(x - h)^2 + k$

vertex: (h, k)

axis: $x = h$

Triangle Inequality

The length of any side in a triangle is between the absolute value of the difference and the sum of the other two sides, i.e.,

$$|a - b| < c < a + b$$

for sides a, b, and c.

Factoring Patterns

Difference of Two Squares (D.O.T.S.):

$x^2 - y^2 = (x + y)(x - y)$

$(x - y)^2 = x^2 - 2xy + y^2$

$(x + y)^2 = x^2 + 2xy + y^2$

Midpoint

The x (or y) value of the midpoint is the average of the x (or y) value of two points.

Distance

To find the distance between two points, draw a right triangle and use the Pythagorean theorem.

Triangle

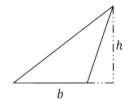
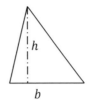

$$A = \frac{bh}{2}$$

Trapezoid

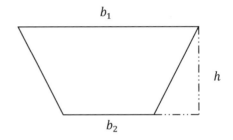

$$A = \frac{(b_1 + b_2)h}{2}$$

Parallelogram

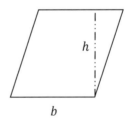

$$A = bh$$

Trig Identities

$$\sin^2\theta + \cos^2\theta = 1$$

$$\tan\theta = \frac{\sin\theta}{\cos\theta}$$

COMPLEX NUMBERS

$i = \sqrt{-1}$ $i^0 = 1$

$i^1 = i$ $i^2 = -1$

$i^3 = -i$ $i^4 = 1$

LOGARITHMS

$$b^a = x \ \leftrightarrow \ \log_b x = a$$

$\log_b xy = \log_b x + \log_b y$ $\log x = \log_{10} x$

$\log_b \dfrac{x}{y} = \log_b x - \log_b y$ $\log_b b = 1$

$\log_b 1 = 0$

$\log_b x^y = y\log_b x$ $\log_b b^n = n$

EQUATION OF A CIRCLE

$$(x - h)^2 + (y - k)^2 = r^2$$

center: (h, k)

radius: r

QUADRATIC FORMULA

$$ax^2 + bx + c = 0$$

$$x = \frac{-b \pm \sqrt{b^2 - 4ac}}{2a}$$

POLYNOMIALS

If $(x - a)$ is a factor of the polynomial $p(x)$, then $p(a) = 0$.

If $p(a) = 0$, then $(x - a)$ is a factor of $p(x)$.

SOH-CAH-TOA

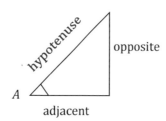

$$\sin A = \frac{opp}{hyp} \quad \cos A = \frac{adj}{hyp} \quad \tan A = \frac{opp}{adj}$$

TRIGONOMETRIC LAWS

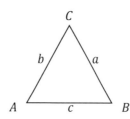

Law of sines:

$$\frac{a}{\sin A} = \frac{b}{\sin B} = \frac{c}{\sin C}$$

Law of cosines:

$$c^2 = a^2 + b^2 - 2ab \cos C$$

UNIT CIRCLE

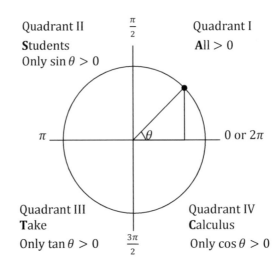

Quadrant II
Students
Only $\sin \theta > 0$

$\frac{\pi}{2}$

Quadrant I
All > 0

π

θ

0 or 2π

Quadrant III
Take
Only $\tan \theta > 0$

$\frac{3\pi}{2}$

Quadrant IV
Calculus
Only $\cos \theta > 0$

180 degrees = π radians

d degrees = $d \cdot \frac{\pi}{180}$ radians

r radians = $r \cdot \frac{180}{\pi}$ degrees

TRIGONOMETRIC FUNCTIONS

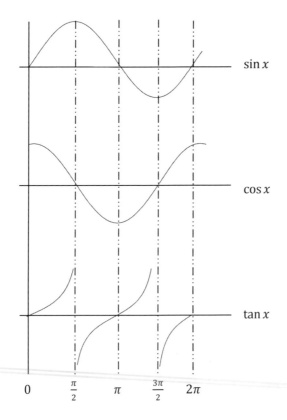

$\sin x$

$\cos x$

$\tan x$

0      $\frac{\pi}{2}$ π $\frac{3\pi}{2}$ 2π

IMPORTANT TRIG DEFINITIONS

Amplitude: half vertical distance between "crest" and "trough."

Period: length over which a function repeats.
(e.g. $\sin x$ has a period of 2π.)

Even function:
$$f(-x) = f(x) \quad (\cos x)$$

Odd function:
$$f(-x) = -f(x) \quad (\sin x)$$

CHAPTER 3: READING

Reading Approaches: ACT

INTRODUCTION

The ACT Reading section can be an exercise in frustrating simplicity. On the one hand, the passages tend to be straightforward, and do not employ sophisticated arguments or vocabulary. On the other hand, the passages are quite lengthy, requiring test-takers to get through a lot of information quickly and retain a good amount of it as well. Different students have different reading speeds, and different retention abilities, so strategies will vary somewhat from student to student. Nevertheless, all students should be intimately familiar with the information and approaches given below. Consult with your academic coach to find which of these approaches are best suited to you.

THE FOUR GENRES

The ACT Reading section always includes four passages from four different genres in the following order:

o *Literary Narrative (formerly known as Prose Fiction)*—usually explores the interactions of two or more characters and depends heavily on dialogue. While this is the least straightforward of the passages, some students are attracted to the strong narrative and deeper attention to language, which helps to keep them interested. Others find it difficult to locate the information because, unlike with the essay, this passage does not tend to feature either substantial paragraphs or topic sentences. In addition, the questions themselves usually do not contain as many line-references or other "locators" (see below) as those for other passages.

o *Social Science*—a persuasive essay on topics of communal interest, including government, history, environmental issues, and so forth. Some students find it easier to work with this type of passage because the paragraphs usually feature topic sentences, and the questions frequently include line-references and other "locators." Other students find the content dry and have trouble reading, processing, and retaining the information it contains.

o *Humanities*—a subjective investigation (often an excerpt from a memoir) of entertainment and the arts, including literature, t.v. shows, music, and so forth. Some students feel drawn to the personal tone of this passage, its subject matter, and the line-references and "locators" in the questions. Other students find the subject matter uninteresting and difficult to understand. Note that when the text is taken from a memoir, it is often indistinguishable from Literary Narrative.

o *Natural Science*—typically an objective exploration of a scientific topic, including anything from dinosaurs to color-perception to snow. This is the most straightforward and logical of the passages, and some students enjoy applying their analytical skills to the subject matter, as well as the fairly high number of line-references and other "locators." Others find the subject matter uninteresting and/or confusing, and have trouble drawing conclusions based on the given information.

LOCATORS

The majority of answers on the ACT Reading are locatable within the text. Anything that helps you quickly locate information is therefore very valuable. Locators include:

o *Line-References*—Specific line numbers from the passage. This is the most direct, and the most important, type of locator.
o *Paragraph Numbers*—While not as specific as a line-reference, this still tells you exactly where to look; it may simply take a little longer to read.
o *Proper Names*—If you are quickly searching through a passage, you can find proper names more easily because they begin with capital letters.
o *Dates*—In general, the passages do not feature many numbers, so these should be fairly easy to locate quickly.

FIND YOUR FAVORITES

Although the four passages always appear in the order given above, you can do them in any order you like. Some students may prefer to begin with the passages they are most comfortable with, leaving their least favorite for last, while others prefer to end on a high note with the passage they find most engaging (and, therefore, can finish the fastest). As you take practice exams and work through homework, you and your tutor can determine what order works best for you.

READ IT FIRST

The questions on the Reading section do not necessarily follow the order of the passage: the first question might discuss something towards the end, the next something towards the beginning of the passage, etc. It is better to read the passage (or some of the passage) *quickly* first, not so much to understand every nuance, but to give yourself a rough idea of what it's about and how its information is organized.

Majority Method vs. Outline Method

For most students who have trouble reading the passages quickly enough to allow them sufficient time to tackle the questions, it often makes sense to read the first 2/3 or 3/4 of the passage and then proceed to the questions. This approach allows students to have a good understanding of the overall theme and tone of the passage and to move onto the questions sooner, and its potentially detrimental effects are minimal: should students encounter a question that deals with a topic they have not encountered earlier in the passage, they will know to look in the last 1/3 or 1/4. Lastly, it helps keep students focused on strategies and time, rather than getting caught up in the reading of the passage itself.

Some students prefer not to read as much before diving into the questions, either because it takes up too much time or because they can more easily remain engaged if they read less. For these students it might make sense to read the first paragraph (the introduction), the topic sentences of each body paragraph, and the last paragraph (the conclusion). This way, the student has a sense of the scope of the essay's argument or narrative and also a sense of where each piece of information is located.

Keep an Eye on the Time

As with the rest of the ACT, time-management on the Reading section is key. Your tutor will work with you to determine which of the following three time plans will work best for you:

- **9, 9, 9, 8:** If you are a fairly quick reader, you might elect to spend approximately 9 minutes on the first three passages, and 8 minutes on the last one. If you are following this time plan, you should probably spend around 3 minutes reading/skimming the passage, and 5–6 minutes answering the questions.

- **10, 10, 10, 5:** This is the time plan the majority of students employ. In so doing, you should plan on spending about 4 minutes reading each of the first 3 passages, and approximately 6 minutes answering the questions. When you get to the last passage, and have only 5 minutes left for the last 10 questions, you should NOT read the passage first—there simply isn't enough time. Instead, either read the topic sentence of each paragraph and then go to the questions, or just go to the questions immediately. This is a triage strategy; you're trying to do all that you can to give your full attention to the first three passages, and pick up whatever quick points you can on the last one.

- **11, 11, 11, 2:** If you find that 10 minutes simply isn't enough time for you to get through a passage and its corresponding questions, you might employ this method, devoting your full attention to three of the passages and guessing (randomly if need be) on the last one. Remember to never leave anything blank!

Question Answering Strategies

"Find It" vs. Interpret

Generally speaking, there are two kinds of questions on the Reading section: stated information (sometimes referred to as "find it") and interpretation ("interpret"). As each type corresponds to very different approaches and answers, it's essential when you first read a question, even before you start looking through the answer choices or referring back to the passage, that you establish which type of question you're dealing with. Some students find it useful to put an "S" or an "I" by each question as they're doing them.

Stated Information (a.k.a. "Find it")

These questions, which contain identifying words and phrases such as "state," "indicate," "claim," "argue," "describe," and "according to," have correct answers that appear either word for word, or very close to it, in the passage itself. The challenge lies not in deciphering a particular part of the passage, but in locating a straightforward statement in the passage. In other words, if you can just find the right part of the passage, the answer should be obvious. Precisely because the challenge lies in locating (not interpreting), these types of questions will often not contain line numbers; if they did, they would be too easy.

Interpretation

These questions, which contain identifying words and phrases such as "imply," "infer," "suggest," "best," "most," "primarily," "mainly," "in order to," "characterize," "depict," and "portray" have correct answers that do NOT appear word for word in the passage, and consequently require you to read between the lines or to generalize. Understanding the tone of the passage (before you begin to interpret the content) will often get you to the correct answer more quickly. Ask yourself, "Is the emotion of this part of the passage more positive, negative, or neutral?" Once you have determined the tone—and eliminated any answer choices whose tone is inappropriate, you can start to look for synonyms between the passage and the answer choices. Because the challenge involved with these questions lies primarily in understanding the text on a deeper level, as opposed to locating information, they will often (but not always) contain line-numbers.

 Watch Out! Precisely because interpretation questions will require you to identify tone and synonyms (as opposed to exact language), those answers that quote directly from the passage are likely incorrect. A good rule of thumb to employ is to look for the "Same Meaning, Different Words."

TIER SYSTEM

Although the questions do not occur in order of difficulty, you can learn to quickly identify how easy or hard a question is based on how it is phrased and whether it includes locators. Within each passage, do all the easy questions first, then the medium, then, if you have time, the hard ones. To some degree, difficulty is subjective, so you and your tutor might develop a plan different from the one below; that being said, what follows is a general guideline for most students.

Easy

For most students, the greatest difficulty often lies in simply finding information; therefore, they often choose to first attempt those questions that contain locators, such as line-references, paragraph numbers, proper names, and dates, regardless of whether it's a stated information or an interpretation question.

 Watch Out! Some questions may point to line numbers that cover a long section of text, use the word "refers," or provide you with answer choices that each contain line numbers; while these are certainly direct locators, they very often will require you to spend a great deal of time either attempting to re-skim a lot of text or look in many different areas. These are NOT easy questions, and you might well want to save them for later. Note as well that some questions that use the word "refers," and ask you to compare some specific line numbers with some other, unspecified section of the text, can also prove difficult; therefore you should approach "refers" questions with a little caution.

Medium
These are of two kinds:

1. Stated information questions that do not provide a locator. While the answers to these may be straightforward, without a locator it might take a good amount of time for you to locate the necessary information.
2. Questions that deal with the passage as a whole. Note that these are interpretation questions, which means you'll need to consider tone and larger ideas rather than a specific section of text. They may include language such as "the primary purpose of the passage," "the point of view of the passage," and so forth.

Hard:

Other than the kind mentioned in the Watch Out! note above, these fall into three general categories.

1. Inference questions that do not have locators. Not only do these questions not tell you where to look, but even when you do find the right part of the passage, you'll still need to do some interpretation. This is the worst of both worlds.

2. Questions that use the words NOT, LEAST, or EXCEPT and do not provide locators. Not only do these questions require you to reverse your usual strategy of finding the most appropriate answer (since for these, it is the most "wrong" answer that is actually the correct one), but they also tend to take a great deal of time. For example, in the question, "The author mentions all of the following in the passage EXCEPT," we have no way of anticipating what the correct answer might be, and therefore have no other choice than to slowly eliminate one answer after another.

3. Questions that ask about the sequence of events within the passage. Often when a question asks "Which of the following occurs first in the passage," it's a bit of a trick question, as the question is referring to the order in which the events *occur*, not the order in which they *appear*. In fact, the vast majority of the time, you can be sure that whatever occurs first in the passage will *not* be what appear first. But even with that it mind, it can be very time-consuming to go through and use process of elimination to determine the correct answer.

Hardest

Most students will either want to avoid these altogether (guess and move on) or save them for last. Luckily, these question types tend to appear less frequently.

o Questions that refer to large swaths of text or to two or more different line references (either within the question itself or the answer choices)

o Questions whose answer choices are lists with only a slight amount of variation among them (e.g., answer choice A) "Two dogs, three kittens, and four possums, B) three dogs, 1 kitten, and two possums)

o Additional/Analogous questions—these ask you to compare some outside information or point of view to what is contained within the passage (e.g., "Keats once wrote that 'beauty is truth'; would the author of this passage agree or disagree?)

READING STRATEGIES

While reading, it is always extremely helpful to keep your pencil moving. It helps you highlight important information and remain focused on what you are reading. But what should you be underlining, circling, etc.?

MAP THE PASSAGE (TONE & STRUCTURE)

When reading through a passage, it's all too easy to get caught up in the particular information it contains, and while it's certainly important for you determine what the passage is about, you'll want to simultaneously identify two other key concepts as you read:

- **Tone:** This is the author's emotion. Ask yourself if the author is praising, criticizing, or simply giving information, i.e., if the tone is, respectively, positive, negative, or neutral. This is a vital step because the tone of the passage will often match the tone of the correct answer. Note that, for the most part, the tone of the passage will be consistent throughout—if the author/narrator is happy at the beginning, they're likely to stay that way. Be sure to look for words that convey emotions, be they positive or negative (or the lack of such words). In addition, if you've read the passage but are still struggling to determine the tone, try re-reading the last paragraph; often that's where the author/narrator will make themselves even plainer than they have previously.
- **Structure:** Typically, the passages on this test proceed from the general to the specific. Often, they will discuss some broad phenomenon and then shift to a discussion of one particular understanding of or approach to it. As you read through the passage, keep track of any dramatic shifts, be it from the general to the specific, one setting or timeframe to another, or between perspectives.

CREST

In addition to tone and structure, there are five patterns that you should look out for, as they tend to indicate which parts of the passage the questions will refer back to:

C: Change/comparison/contrast—whenever the setting or time of the passage changes, a big shift in the argument, a comparison between two or more parties, or a contrast word ("but," "yet," "however," etc.).

R: Repetition—any time a word, or some form of the same word, appears in close proximity.

E: Emotional Response/opinion—when an author or a character has an emotional reaction to an event, or when an author or speaker offers an opinion in what is otherwise an informational passage (e.g., the Natural Science passage).

S: Strange/specialized language—this could be figurative language (metaphor, simile, etc.), dense imagery, or the definition of a term from a particular field (e.g., music, biology, etc.)

T: Time words—these could be years, seasons, or words that also function as contrast words (e.g., "now").

Depending on your reading speed and ability to focus on more than one thing at once, it might prove difficult, or even unproductive, to track all of CREST down. Observing these patterns is in no way meant to substitute for solid reading practices such as identifying theme and tone, paraphrasing, and so forth. But noting these patterns and marking them as much as you can while still maintaining your overall focus will help you to understand what information is more important and therefore more likely to be referred to by the questions.

 Watch Out! If you notice a large number of dates, specialized language, etc., you should probably stop marking them—otherwise your passage will have so many notes that it will a) be difficult to read and b) impossible to determine which areas are more significant than others.

Answers & Guessing

Anticipate

Every time you read a question, ask yourself whether it's a stated information or interpretation question, as this will help you to determine whether you should be looking, respectively, for quoted material or tone/synonyms/larger ideas. You should also evaluate the difficulty level of the question. If it appears to be easy, go ahead and tackle it. More difficult? Consider saving it for later.

Look Through the Answers First

After you read a question, but before you refer back to the passage, you should always quickly look through the answer choices for two reasons:

1. They will give you a better sense of what kind of information the question is investigating (and, if you recall the part of the passage that deals with that information, a sense of where you might want to look).

2. You can use simple logic or outside information to identify any answer choices that **by definition** are connected to the answer choices. On 4–5 questions on almost every test, simple information and/or logic will help you to eliminate two or more answer choices. For example, if a question uses the word "efficiency," an answer choice that contains the phrase "without waste" should automatically be more attractive to you. Keep in mind that the Reading is not, for the most part, a trick test. If you know an answer, or see an answer that seems likely based on your general understanding of the real world, it will nearly always be right. Trust your instincts, and go with what seems most reasonable. Note that if you don't have time to check answers to these types of questions, don't worry about it—you can guess with confidence and move on.

The Alpha and the Omega

For most stated information questions, the challenge lies simply in locating the right part of the passage. There's no one correct way to do this, but there are a couple important rules of thumb to keep in mind. Because a high number of ACT questions focus on either *the first paragraph* (introduction) *or the last paragraph* (conclusion) of the passage, try to read those just a bit more carefully, and to check there first if you can't recall where to find a piece of information. If you strike out there, try the first few and last few lines of each paragraph—80% of the time, looking in these locations will prove fruitful.

Private Prep Tactic: If you are having a very difficult time understanding a passage, focus more on the topic sentences than on the middles of the paragraphs. These first sentences can not only provide a quick, convenient introduction to the content of each paragraph, but can also indicate how that paragraph functions in the passage as a whole. If a topic sentence contains a contrast word, pay extra close attention, as this might indicate a larger structural shift in the passage. Note that the Literary Narrative passage, being the most literary, often doesn't have topic sentences, which means you might have to rely more heavily on your annotation to help you map out the passage.

Think Big:

The ACT often favors more general answers over more specific ones. This is especially true on interpretation questions, although it occasionally proves fruitful on stated information questions.

Middle of the Road

The majority of correct answers on the Reading are moderate in tone; you should therefore, in general, avoid answer choices that are extremely positive or negative.

Test the Twins:

When two answer choices are notably more similar to each other than to the remaining answer choices, chances are good that one of them is the correct answer; very often, the more moderate one is right (see Middle of the Road).

Go with the Genre

Sometimes the type of passage you're reading can suggest a correct answer:

1. Literary Narrative answers tend to be less literal (and more figurative).
2. Social Science answers often focus more on the effect on people of a phenomenon than on the phenomenon itself.
3. Humanities answers, like those for Literary Narrative, are often more figurative.
4. Natural Science answers usually deal more with how scientists interpret evidence than on the evidence itself. Correct answers therefore tend to favor opinions over facts, and stress that our understanding of the universe is limited and often aided by fortunate accidents.

By Definition

As mentioned above, 4–5 questions on every test will allow you to use fairly common outside knowledge and/or basic logic to at least eliminate a couple of answer choices. If an answer choice seems much more likely, irrespective of the passage itself, chances are high that it's correct. For example, if a question asks about efficiency, and one of the answer choices mentions "not wasting energy," it's a fair bet that it's the correct one.

 Private Prep Tactic: Look for answer choices that, by definition, have something to do with the concepts included in the question *before* you look back to the passage. This can help you determine which answer choices you should investigate first.

Politically Correct

Correct answers on this section will never say something negative or make any statement that might even be construed as offensive about any group of people, be it African Americans, ethnic minorities, or women working in a traditionally male role (e.g., as doctors or scientists). You should feel comfortable immediately eliminating any answer choice that does so.

What's the Purpose of this Paragraph?

Why would a question single out one paragraph over others? More often than not, it's because it serves a purpose different from those around it, and consequently correct answers to questions that ask for the purpose of a paragraph will refer to some kind of change or shift in the discussion.

EXCEPTIONAL answers:

IF a LEAST/NOT/EXCEPT question features an answer choice that contains a word or phrase from the question itself, chances are high that that answer choice is the correct one (For example, if a question asks "All of the following are sold at Gary's Banana Stand EXCEPT:... and the word "bananas" appears in an answer choice, that one is very likely right.)

AND FINALLY!

While every passage is different, there are some common trends we've observed among correct answers across several tests. Drawing on these trends, while far from guaranteeing a correct answer or serving as a substitute for referring back to the passage, can nevertheless give you an edge if you're going to guess.

- **It's Not Here!** What's a great way to get a test-taker to spend all of his or her time searching for an answer in the passage? Have the correct answer be "this information is not included in the passage." More often than not, if this is an answer choice, it's the right one.
- **Hug a Tree:** Many correct answers involve man doing harm to the environment, or attempting to find ways not to. Others involve returning to an existence that is more in touch with nature.
- **We Don't Know everything:** Correct answers often mention that our understanding of a subject is limited and we still have much to learn.
- **Stuff Just Happens:** Several correct answers over the last few years have referred to the fact that people often make discoveries accidentally, whether it's a piece of art or a scientific phenomenon.
- **Fact vs. Opinion:** Particularly on the Natural Science passage, it is common for correct answers to refer to opinions rather than facts.
- **People Don't Like Change:** Most people are resistant to changes in their environments or ways of thinking, and correct answers often reflect this.

Keep It Moving

You have less than 1 minute total for each question. If you find yourself spending too much time on a particular question, take an educated guess and move on. It's a good idea to circle the ones you're not sure about, so that you can go back and check over them at the very end if you have the time to do so. However, keep in mind the next approach:

Don't Flip-Flop

On the math section of the test, you can check at least some of your answers with the help of your calculator. But on the Reading, you have no such tool to fall back on, so trust your first instincts for two reasons: 1. First guesses are more often correct than second-guesses; and 2. Going back to change answers takes up valuable time that could be used to work on other problems. Unless you see that you have made a clear mistake, go with your first choice.

CHAPTER 4: SCIENCE

Section Overview

INTRODUCTION

The ACT Science section is arguably one of the most misunderstood sections on any standardized test. Although it requires a basic high-school level understanding of the sciences, the majority of its passages deal with graduate-level experiments and ideas. It is not your job to intimately comprehend these concepts, but to use interpretation and deduction to observe patterns and make sense of data.

The 40 questions of the Science section are divided into 6 or 7 passages. While the passages themselves are in no particular order of type or difficulty, the questions in each passage go from easiest to hardest, with the last question of each passage being generally far more difficult than those that precede it.

Because the Science is always the last section of the ACT (with the exception of the essay), many students feel tired before they even start it. Being well versed in the format of the section can at least help you to approach it in a calm, strategic fashion. The section, which is only 35 minutes long, comprises:

- 40 questions
- 6 or 7 total passages
- 2-3 Data Interpretation passages
- 2-3 Research Summary passages
- 1 Conflicting Viewpoints passage

Data Interpretation

The Data Interpretation passages each contain several tables and figures. To do well on these passages, you must interpret the tables and figures with high accuracy. This means locating data, identifying trends, and drawing connections between or among multiple figures. Students typically find these passages somewhat easier than others, so be sure to take full advantage of the opportunity to rack up as many quick, easy points as possible.

Research Summary

The Research Summary passages each contain an overview of a laboratory experiment along with questions that test your understanding of the scientific method. As you progress through the questions and the difficulty increases, try to focus on what the individual studies are investigating, and how they compare to one another. Look for phrases such as "most likely" to identify those questions that might require you to draw a conclusion from a hypothetical scenario.

Conflicting Viewpoints

The Conflicting Viewpoints passage is one students typically dislike because it tends to involve reading more text, even while it may also include figures, tables, and so forth. Your tutor will help you decide whether you should tackle this kind of passage as you encounter it or should save it for later or last. This type of passage tests your interpretation of two or more scientists/students/researchers debating a topic. To do well on this passage, you will need to use as much deduction and interpretation as you did for other passages but will also have to read through and analyze text quickly and sometimes think on multiple levels. It is often useful to find key phrases in the questions, find them in the passage, then find them in the answer choices. As you progress through the passage, try to summarize, in simple terms, each person's argument; this will make it easier for you to compare and contrast them.

Basic Strategies

(NOTE: Refer to Chapter 1 of *For the Love of ACT Science* for further explanation of basic strategies.)

DO NOT READ THE PASSAGES FIRST

- It is not necessary to read and understand the passages before tackling the questions. In fact, reading the passages first can often make you more confused. Instead, each time you turn to a new science passage, follow this strategy:
- In the first few seconds, rapidly skim the passage and the questions to decide whether you should attempt the passage now or save it for later.
- Jump straight to the first question and read it for keywords and phrases directing you to specific studies, experiments, tables, or figures.
- Read the answer choices before trying to find the correct answer in the passage. Look for important features such as units and keywords, all of which can give you an advantage in finding the correct answer.
- Finally, look back at the passage and locate the relevant evidence that allows you to either choose the correct answer directly or by process of elimination; then go on to the next question.
- Be mindful not to spend too much time on any single question. All the questions are worth the same number of points, yet some are markedly less difficult than others, so you want to make sure you get a fair shot at all the easier ones. If a question is taking too much time, put a big circle around it, guess from the choices you haven't yet eliminated, and move on. You can come back to it later if you have time.

ORIENT YOURSELF

Most Science questions refer to information that can be found in tables, charts, graphs, or, occasionally, the text. The most common mistake on the Science test (and primary reason for wasted time) is looking in the wrong place: at the wrong table, wrong axis, wrong row, etc.

 Private Prep Tactic: Use the two-finger method to keep yourself oriented: use one finger to read the question, the other to orient yourself, point by point, on the table, chart, or graph so that you are sure you are looking in the right place.

 Watch Out! Be careful with headings, as their placement varies. Sometimes the title for a table, chart, or graph will be above, sometimes below. Look at the entire page to make sure you're looking at the right place.

GET MESSY

Mark up the passages as much as you like to make the information in the passages easier to understand. For instance, if data in a chart, table, or figure are not in order from least to greatest or greatest to least, then put them in order by numbering them 1, 2, 3, 4, etc. Once you have done so, ask yourself if there is a pattern (are values increasing? decreasing? increasing and then decreasing?). If a value provided in a question is out of the range included in a chart or graph, feel free to extend the lines of the graph to include this new value; try whenever you can to make answering questions a visual—and tactile—experience.

 Private Prep Tactic: In order not to get lost, use easy-to-read symbols (such as arrows, plusses and minuses, and greater-than and less-than signs) to highlight information as you go. This holds for questions too: mark words such as "greater," "less," "increase," "decrease," etc. with symbols wherever you see them in a question or answer statement.
Even though you're not allowed to use a calculator on the Science section, you may sometimes have to do basic math. Do not panic! Usually an estimate or range is fine.

ONE LAST THING...

The last question of each passage, which is often the hardest, tends to explore the scientific method and/or inverse relationships. Questions in the former category often include phrases such as "most likely" or "suppose a new experiment were conducted" and may require you to draw conclusions in the absence of data, whereas questions in the latter category, which often refer back to data in the text and/or figures, will usually require you to untangle an inverse relationship, i.e., one in which one variable increases as another decreases.

If you find yourself lingering on the last question of a section, remember that such questions are generally significantly harder than other questions in a passage and that you are better off taking a quick educated guess and moving on rather than sacrifice the easy points that lie ahead.

* Refer to Chapter 4 in *For the Love of ACT Science* for further review on last questions.

Advanced Strategies

YES, YES, NO, NO

Often answer choices have two parts: a logical conclusion followed by a piece of information. Frequently, answer choices A and C will have the same informational section at the end, while answer choices B and D will share a different piece of information. Because it is usually fairly easy to determine which piece of information (A and C or B and D) is the correct one, it is best to do so first; once you have narrowed down the choices by 50%, you can then make the somewhat more difficult determination of which logical conclusion is the correct one.

* Refer to section 2.1 in *For the Love of ACT Science* for further review on Yes, Yes, No, No.

ANTICIPATING THE EXTRA STEP (SESAME STREET TACTIC)

Last questions often require exactly two steps. The first step is relatively easy: locate a value in a figure or table. The second step requires a bit more work.: apply an inverse trend from a different study to the value in the first step. However, we can skip this second step by thinking about the structure of the answer choices. Sometimes your initial value splits the answer choices into two groups: answer choices that are higher than your value and answer choices that are lower than your value. If you did the question correctly there will be one answer choice in one group and three answer choices in the other group. Whichever group holds only one answer choice is the correct answer.

So why does this work? While the exam is testing your basic knowledge of mathematics and trends, there is usually no need to calculate an exact value. Instead you should determine whether the answer would increase or decrease from its initial value.

* Refer to section 4.2 in *For the Love of ACT Science* for further review on the sesame street tactic.

SCIENTIFIC METHOD

Research summary passages test not only your knowledge of the experiment but of the scientific method; to that end you should familiarize yourself with the terms below:

- o **Constant:** a factor that remains unchanged throughout a trial or experiment.
- o **Independent Variable:** a factor that is purposely changed at the beginning or throughout the course of the experiment.
- o **Dependent Variable:** a factor that changes as a result of changes in the independent variable.
- o **Control Group:** a specimen or material that, unlike the others in an experiment or trial, is not subject to a change in any variable.

Sample experiment

Suppose you are performing an experiment to measure the growth of five plants, each of which is given a different amount of water and sunlight. For the first batch of tests, you hold the amount of sunlight the same for each (sunlight is constant). You give the first plant (the control group) no water and to give every other plant a different amount of water (independent variable). Over time, you record the growth (dependent variable) of each plant.

Note that in the experiment above you did not change both the sunlight and water amount at the same time. Doing so would have made it difficult, if not impossible, to determine what separate effect each factor had on the growth of the plants. Therefore, for any given experiment on the Science section, there is only one independent variable; anything else that could potentially affect the results will be held constant.

 REMINDER! Independent variables (which tend to be nice round numbers) always appear on the x-axis, whereas dependent variables (which tend to fall in uneven increments) always appear on the y-axis. Also note that in tables, independent variables will be in the left-hand column, while dependent variables will be in the columns to the right.

* Refer to Chapter 3 in *For the Love of ACT Science* for further review of the scientific method.

OUTSIDE KNOWLEDGE

More and more, the Science section has begun to include questions that can only be answered correctly by using some outside information. The good news is that this will only happen a few times on any given exam; being able to locate data and interpret trends is much more important. That being said, it's wise to familiarize yourself with a few general scientific definitions and principles.

* Refer to section 4.3 in *For the Love of ACT Science* for further review on outside knowledge.

HAVE THE RIGHT MINDSET

Below is a bullet point list of things to help you attain—and maintain—the right mindset for the Science section:

- o   Deduce, deduce, deduce: Do not attempt to comprehend the experiments or scientists' statements. The passages may present grad-level research, but you are not expected to have a profound understanding of what is taking place.
- o   Think like a scientist: Identify trends, use estimation, and make educated guesses.
- o   Locate key phrases and words in the question and answer choices, then go find them in the passage. Do not look back at the passage waiting for an epiphany— search for specific information.
- o   Though the Conflicting Viewpoints passage is usually text heavy, you should follow the same general procedure as for the other passages: Go straight to the questions, rely on deduction and logic, and read selectively.
- o   The last question of each passage is often the hardest. If you are struggling through a passage, do not waste your time battling through this question. Make an educated guess and move on to the next passage.

CHAPTER 5: ESSAY

Essay Methodology: ACT

INTRODUCTION

Although the ACT Essay is technically "optional," the vast majority of schools require it, so be sure to sign up for the "ACT with Writing." The ACT Essay prompts follow a standard format: they describe an issue and provide three brief "perspectives" on that issue. Students are asked to discuss the points of view given and to present their own point of view.

TIME MANAGEMENT

With only 40 minutes to plan and craft the essay, there is no time to waste. Below is rule of thumb for how students should use their allotted time efficiently:

- **Read:** Spend no more than 5 minutes reading the assignment.
- **Plan:** Spend 6-8 minutes planning the essay and creating a basic outline that includes the thesis statement and 2–3 supporting examples.
- **Write:** A well thought-out and planned essay should take 22–23 minutes to put on paper.
- **Proofread:** Students will have 2–4 minutes to read back over their essay and correct obvious grammatical errors.

 Watch Out! Do not attempt to make large structural changes to the essay while proofreading. Too often this leads to illegible sentences.

ESSAY STRUCTURE

Effective essays are structured like an hourglass—a broad introductory paragraph, specific examples in the body paragraphs, and a broad conclusion to tie the essay together. Students should use two or three examples to support their thesis. However, two fully developed examples are better than three tossed-off ones.

 Private Prep Tactic: Essays that use most (or all) of the space allotted frequently receive a higher score. Use as much of the given space as possible to fully develop your point of view.

THREE GENERAL RULES OF THUMB

1. **Avoid Extreme Language**

   Students often use words such as "all, only, everybody, always, never, must" to emphasize their thesis. Extreme language actually weakens arguments by creating a higher burden of proof. For example, "Creative thinking <u>always</u> has more value in society than analytical analysis." This thesis statement would be stronger if "always" were removed—"Creative thinking has more value in society than analytical analysis."

2. **Avoid Singular Phrases**

   Whenever possible, avoid using singular phrases such as "one" or "a person," as this often leads to lengthy and awkward constructions such as "his or her." Instead, use plurals, such as "people."

3. **Keep Vocab Simple**

   Do not use overly sophisticated vocabulary in an effort to impress your readers. They are weighing the structure and logic of your argument much more than your diction. In addition, using words with which you are not intimately familiar can create awkward or incorrect phrasings.

THESIS STRATEGIES

Strengths and Weaknesses

After reading the prompt, take some time to write out the strengths and weaknesses of each of the three perspectives. These could be things you feel that the perspective gets right, aspects you agree with, holes in the argument, or refutations of the point of view. As you go, see if you can draw connections between what you feel are the strengths of one perspective and the weaknesses of others; those connections will help determine your thesis.

Take a Stand

It is imperative that you develop a point of view. This is a meant to be a persuasive essay. While not technically incorrect, it is more difficult to argue both sides of the coin and offer an alternative view, especially given the time limit.

Examples First

Students will find it much easier to draft the essay if they first allow themselves to thoroughly analyze the three given perspectives and come up with specific examples to illustrate their points of view. How could you possibly know what your thesis statement will be without having considered how you will back it up? Be open to the idea that your argument may not actually be aligned with what you really think--come up with a list of examples on all sides of the issue. Whichever examples are strongest should determine the thesis statement.

Formula of the Opposite

A great way to form a concise and effective introduction for an essay is to follow the Formula of the Opposite. Followed correctly, this will provide students with a solid, three-sentence intro paragraph. The first sentence should directly contradict the statement you plan to make in your thesis. The second sentence should then be the thesis. Finally, the third sentence should wrap it up by teasing the examples you plan to use to prove your thesis statement. This helps keep the intro short and sweet, saving the other good stuff for the body paragraphs where it belongs.

Example: In response to the following prompt—"Automation is generally seen as a sign of progress, but what is lost when we replace humans with machines? Given the accelerating variety and prevalence of intelligent machines, it is worth examining the implications and meaning of their presence in our lives."—a student could write:

Many people would argue that intelligent machines make our lives easier and more prosperous. However, as we transfer more of our industry to machines, many people will begin to find themselves out of work. The dangers of this can be seen through the example of the auto industry in the last century.

EXAMPLES STRATEGIES

Be Specific

Specific examples offer more support than generalizations. On the ACT it is easy to get roped in to using generalizations. For example, a student that uses the example of smart phones to support the thesis "The prevalence of technology like smart phones unites, rather than divides, the human race." An example that simply states "IPhones bring people together" is far less effective than an example of a specific situation where the use of a smart phone aided in making a human connection or improving its users' lives.

Make Connections Clear

Don't assume that the reader has made a connection between your example and thesis because you think it's obvious. Every step of the way, be sure to show how each example supports your thesis.

 Watch Out! Students often get caught spending several sentences explaining their example. The setup for an example should be short and sweet, with the focus relating back to why it supports the thesis.

CONCLUSION STRATEGIES

Broaden Your Horizons

The conclusion is an opportunity to look beyond the thesis and make an even broader statement. For instance, expanding on the example given above, a student might begin a conclusion with the statement: "Modern society has been made undoubtedly better with the use of intelligent machines. We are accustomed to seamlessness and innovation far beyond what our predecessors could have imagined. Yet there is a human cost to all of this. As we proceed down the path of technological enlightenment, we must remain aware of our own humanity and its needs."

Make a Dire Prediction

Since this is a persuasive essay, you might want to make a prediction about what kind of bad things would happen if your point of view were not followed. For instance, expanding on the example given above, a student might write: "If intelligent machines are promoted at the expense of humans' livelihoods, we'll have a nation of underemployed humans and too-powerful machines."

Offer a Solution

Toward the end of your introduction, you can describe how implementing some strategy that is in line with your thesis will help to counteract or overcome problems that would arise from not following your point of view. For instance, expanding on the example given above, a student might write: "If machines are given more limited uses, then humans will remain in control and can better use that technology to navigate the problems of the next century."

Essay Score Guide: ACT

SAMPLE QUESTION:

Teaching and Expertise

The traditional model of education is focused on a qualified teacher who controls the curriculum entirely. The premise is that a teacher by definition possesses greater knowledge of a subject than her students, who are there to benefit from her advanced understanding. But recent studies suggest that students learn better when given the task of teaching a specific concept to their peers. This result has been attributed to the sense of responsibility and collaboration students feel when put in a position to teach. Should students play a role in teaching their peers? How should we think about the responsibilities of both teachers and students?

Read and carefully consider these perspectives. Each suggests a particular way of thinking about teaching and expertise.

Perspective 1	Perspective 2	Perspective 3
By definition, students do not possess the knowledge and skills necessary to teach. The best way for students to learn is under the care of a trained and qualified teacher.	Students learn best when taking responsibility for their own education. The best way to encourage this is to oblige students to help teach their peers.	Various forms of collaboration between teachers and students should be explored. Education is a process of experimentation and creation that requires new approaches.

Essay Score: 1

Ideas and Analysis: Score – 1

Organization: Score – 1

Development and Support: Score – 1

Language Use and Conventions: Score – 1

Teachers are supposed to be better at teaching then students because they go to school for it but also students could teach some stuff if they wanted. That will probably take longer and not be full of very great information but they could try. Alot of the times kids would know some facts that they could teach othertimes they could be having trouble but maybe someone could help. Whatever is best for kids should be what we all do so if we could find that out for sure that would be the right thing to do for teachers' and kids both. If it ends up wasting time then the teacher would know not to do it again or alot of the time. Kids need a good education to do good things with there life so they should get the best education so they can have better jobs and a happy life.

Why this essay received a score of 1:
This essay lacks a thesis and fails to actively analyze any of the three perspectives provided in the prompt. Instead, the author makes many broad claims without providing logical evidence to support his or her ideas. The single-paragraph-setup lacks logical organization, and the essay contains many spelling and grammar errors.

ESSAY SCORE: 2

Ideas and Analysis: Score – 2   Organization: Score – 2

Development and Support: Score – 2   Language Use and Conventions: Score – 2

Should students be able to teach sometimes in school? I believe they should not for many reasons. Kids are not as smart as teachers because teachers have already graduated and gone to school. So it would not help for a student to teach about things if the teacher knows more about it.

Students can tell the class information that is not right and then the teacher would have to spend more time teaching the right thing later. If classes have to hear the same stuff over and over they can get confused and not know what is right and can not remember what was the good information vs. what was the bad info.

Also, students have always been students and teachers have always been teachers. Did Einstein teach a class about the Great Gatsby when he was in school? I bet no. He turned out fine and he had a teacher teaching him. If its' good enough for Einstein, its' good enough for us.

And teaching is stressful. If I was the student, I would not want to teach my friends about something because it would give me anxiety and take alot of work. That is a teachers' job so the teacher should be doing all of that work. A teacher controls a class and tells them new information so they can learn – not students. Also if my friend was teaching my class I don't think I could take them seriously.

In conclusion, teachers should teach and students should learn. Teachers are better at it and it would make students nervous. Also they would learn incorrect information and get confused easily. Still, education is important and we should continue talking about it.

Why this essay received a score of 2:
This essay provides more structure and organization than the first example, but it still fails to engage with either the prompt or the provided perspectives in a substantial way. The author again makes broad claims that are not supported by any logical evidence and often repeats a single claim multiple times. Those claims are also not always clearly related to the essay's thesis, bringing their relevance into question. The essay contains both spelling and grammatical mistakes, as well as ambiguous and unclear language.

Essay Score: 3

Idea Analysis: Score – 3

Organization: Score – 3

Development and Support: Score – 3

Language Use and Conventions: Score – 3

Education is a very important part of society today. It lays the foundation for many things that come later in life including: college, jobs, and more. A good education is necessary to succeed, so we should educate kids in the best way, whether that is learning from a teacher or learning from other students. Both sides have pros and cons, which I will discuss below.

Some people believe that students will not be good at teaching they're peers, wasting precious learning time. Most schools have to stick to a very strict schedule in order to cover all of the material for the year so they may run out of time if teachers have to reteach information that students incorrectly taught they're peers. Which leads me to my next point: students may not know all of the information as well as teachers, so then they would teach incorrect facts to the class. That would be very confusing and not help the learning process.

Other people believe that students can learn valuable lessons from teaching. To go up in front of a class to teach, a student would have to research a topic and figure out how to best tell the class about it. That means they would learn about a new topic and learn how to present that information. Public speaking would also be a part of that. And some students might be more likely to listen to a friend instead of a teacher since they have a more personal relationship.

In school, sometimes people experiment with this balance to find new ideas. If we explore different ways of students interacting with other students and with teachers, new forms of collaboration might happen. New approaches may be discovered, leading everyone to an even better option.

All in all, many people discuss the best way to educate kids. Some believe that students need to teach sometimes, and other people believe it is a waste of time. Both opinions have valid points that should be taken into consideration. Maybe some teachers prefer one method over a different one. Either way, we should all do our best to give kids the best education.

Why this essay received a score of 3:
While this essay does have a clear thesis at the end of the first paragraph, its wording is ambiguous and attempts to agree with both sides of the argument rather than take a stand for a single idea. This sets the author up to vaguely agree with all of the provided perspectives rather than to deal with them on a substantial level, though the attempt to address all perspectives marks a step above the preceding essays. The essay attempts to provide some logical evidence, as can be seen in the lists and examples provided, but that evidence does not clearly demonstrate the intended point or relate back to the thesis. The essay contains some spelling and grammatical mistakes throughout and could greatly benefit from more precise and advanced wording.

Essay Score: 4

Ideas and Analysis: Score – 4   Organization: Score – 4

Development and Support: Score – 4   Language Use and Conventions: Score – 4

As society begins to analyze our educational system, many have pushed to have students teach their peers more often. Though this may be a great tool for teachers, various forms of collaboration between teachers, students, and peers would have the most benefits for students. Some students may have trouble listening to lecture style lessons from teachers all day. Others may have trouble taking their friend seriously when they're teaching the class. Finding a balance between those two, as well as new learning opportunities, would best serve students.

The traditional way to teach a classroom is to have a smart knowledgeable teacher telling them what they need to know. This form has worked since schooling has existed, and lots of people have come out of those systems being very intellectual and smart. However, not all students learn best in these conditions. Some students need visuals to help them learn and some prefer personal research projects. Furthermore, even though all teachers have attended school and know the material, not all teachers have a high skillset in terms of teaching. Some may be boring to listen to while others may be impatient when explaining a topic in more than one way when a student cannot understand. Having a knowledgeable teacher does not ensure that all students will learn best in a teacher-run classroom environment.

Still, a classroom that relies only on students teaching their peers is unrealistic. Students do not know as much about a given topic as a teacher since they have not yet attended as much school as their teacher. That means they may teach their peers incorrect information, which would cause many problems. Classroom time would be wasted when teachers have to correct their peer leaders, students would be confused as to which information was correct, and students might not take their peers seriously. There may even be students who do not want to present information to their peers.

The only feasible answer is to find a balance between multiple teaching styles, which would require experimentation in each classroom. Teachers want to teach their classes to the best of their abilities, so most of them would likely be open to trying different forms of collaboration in the classroom. They may find that some forms of teaching work better than others for a given subject. Perhaps they may assign individualized projects to each student who can then present, or "teach," this new information to the class. Students all have different learning styles, and giving teachers room to experiment would help more of these students then sticking to a rigid form of teacher or student-led classrooms.

Why this essay received a score of 4:
The introductory paragraph of this essay contains a clear thesis and properly lays out the organization of the essay's body paragraphs. While not explicitly stated, the essay does engage with each of the three perspectives provided in the prompt. Some claims lack logical supporting evidence, but most are related back to the thesis in some way. Language throughout the essay is more precise than that of the lower scoring essays, and less grammatical and spelling mistakes are present.

ESSAY SCORE: 5

Ideas and Analysis: Score – 5

Organization: Score – 5

Development and Support: Score – 5

Language Use and Conventions: Score – 5

Education is an important topic of conversation; legislators, parents, and researchers try to find the most beneficial teaching methods to best serve our youth. A new study suggested that students benefit most from taking responsibility for their own education – specifically, when teaching their peers. However, some believe that peer-to-peer teaching wastes precious schooling hours and leaves children with incorrect or poorly explained information. These concerns are outweighed by the benefits gained through such teaching methods. Societies should employ any and all teaching methods that prove fruitful to various learning styles.

Those who believe that only qualified teachers should teach within classrooms discuss numerous issues with peer-to-peer teaching. Some state that students are likely to have unreliable information that will then be passed down to their peers, causing confusion and misinformation. While this may be true, it seems unrealistic to assume that a trained teacher would not correct inaccuracies. All peer-to-peer teaching must be monitored in some way to guarantee accuracy, but that would likely be an existing concern for teachers. Others then claim that this correction process wastes valuable schooling hours, leaving students behind and wanting for information. Many teaching methods that are currently employed, however, have similar defects: a student may memorize the spelling of "Massachusetts" incorrectly at home when studying for a spelling test but part of their learning process includes teacher-led corrections in the classroom. The point of research is to ensure that one style of teaching or learning is not vastly less effective or useful than another, not to ensure that all teaching methods are perfect.

The way in which society views education and the learning process is constantly changing. A student deemed unsuccessful one hundred years ago may now be diagnosed with a learning disability or benefit from an alternative learning process. Teachers utilize songs, personal projects, kinesthetic exercises, and technology to help students with various learning styles obtain the best education possible. Why, then, are we trying to limit the growth and expansion of teaching techniques? Students have truely benefited from these other teaching techniques, especially students with learning disabilities or alternative learning styles. Peer-to-peer teaching can be yet another tool for teachers to use, ensuring that they reach as many students as they possibly can.

Though I'm no expert, I imagine that peer-to-peer teaching does have many positive affects. As students research a topic, they learn skills that they'll need in any college or university:

finding reliable sources, differentiating between paraphrasing and summarizing, etc. Furthermore, students would then need to take that information and decide how to best present it to a class. This may prove especially difficult for shy students, but all students must eventually do some sort of required public speaking – whether it is a job interview or giving a presentation at work. Then, students would be able to receive constructive criticism from their teachers and better their lessons – yet another skill that will come in handy for the rest of their lives.

Overall, the view of how we teach children is changing. We now know that students learn in a multitude of ways, and there are many different teaching styles that can help different types of learners. We should work as a society to perfect these techniques, which will require constant research and experimentation within the classroom. The benefits of these new techniques outweigh their shortcomings.

Why this essay received a score of 5:
This essay contains a clear thesis that is then used as a lens through which the author evaluates each of the perspectives provided in the prompt. The argument follows a logical organization and uses clear and specific examples to illustrate each point. The author relates each new point back to the essay's thesis and also acknowledges counterarguments. The essay showcases varied word choice and sentence structure throughout. Although the essay contains occasional grammatical and spelling mistakes, they do not detract from the overall purpose and content of the essay.

ESSAY SCORE: 6

Ideas and Analysis: Score – 6

Organization: Score – 6

Development and Support: Score – 6

Language Use and Conventions: Score – 6

The traditional connotation of school shows a teacher standing in front of a classroom, molding the minds of society's youth. With new research and pedagogy, however, this model is constantly in flux. Many teachers now utilize a myriad of teaching techniques to target students with a variety of learning capabilities and preferences. Still, there are those who prefer the traditional model. Pushback on educational innovations often center around fears of misinformation, wasted time, and a lack of structure. Yet without these innovations, how can we push society to grow more, learn more, and stay relevant? Rather than ignore new research, we should instead insist that teachers remain properly trained in new pedagogy – in this case, letting students teach one another.

Advances in educational pedagogy are more common than ever. Society holds education in the highest regard, which has led many research institutes to ask exactly how teachers can best serve our students. Innovations that have come out of such research include the realization that different students respond to different teaching methods. Logic follows, then, that a successful teacher in today's school would employ more than one of these methods. For example, some subjects may be best taught in a lecture setting while others can be turned into songs, physical activities, proofs, or visual projects. A chemistry class might learn about the "mole" measurement by each coming up with an imaginative illustration using real life models: what percentage of our planet would be covered in a mole of cars? A fifth-grade classroom may learn the names of all fifty states with a song. Each method will reach a different student in a different way, ensuring that all students have the opportunity to learn.

Still, none of these methods are full proof. Were all lessons to be taught by students to students, misinformation would become rampant and lessons that usually take hours may take days. Should we then consider this mode of teaching a failure? By no means. Each method of teaching does not prove successful on its own. Even after the research has been completed, various teachers could employ a single mode of teaching in a million different ways. While no single method can reach every student every time it is employed, there must be a way to better assure correct utilization and implementation.

For that reason, teacher trainings explaining any innovations in pedagogy are imperative in creating successful learning environments. Yes, teachers will still need to work with their students and experiment to find an exact balance, but researchers and training groups could help lessen this transitional time. Successful teachers not only use a variety of methods, but they're also aware of which methods best serve which students, and when those methods should be employed. Songs, for instance, are quite useful with route memorization. Term papers, however, are better suited to display a certain kind of thought process. Each and every teaching mode that research has deemed successful should and can be used in our current education system, so long as teachers know how to properly utilize them.

It is a society's responsibility to teach its youth to the best of its abilities. Research plays a large role in this balance, yet it's not enough. To properly translate research into successful teaching, educators require continuous education in all new teaching methods. Should we fail to help our teachers utilize all of this new information, we may fall behind the rest of the world. Education ensures that today's youth can become tomorrow's leaders, and without proper execution, that process is a muddy road to success.

Why this essay received a score of 6:
The thesis of this essay creates a new and specific lens through which the author examines each of the provided perspectives. The essay is clearly organized, and each new claim is supported with a clear and logical example. Counterarguments are taken into account, and each point seamlessly relates back to the essay's thesis. The essay contains specific, varied vocabulary and sentence structure, all while maintaining minimal grammatical and spelling mistakes. The author expresses ideas beyond the limits of the provided perspectives, but still engages with each one on a meaningful level.

CHAPTER 6: PERFORMANCE PREP

MENTAL PREPARATION FOR TEST TAKING

HOMEWORK ASSIGNMENTS

CHAPTER 7: STUDENT PAGES

HOMEWORK ASSIGNMENTS

NOTES

ABOUT PRIVATE PREP

Private Prep is a premier educational services company offering individually customized lessons for a wide range of Pre-K through college-level subjects, executive functioning, standardized test prep, and college admissions consulting. Each family works with a personal Education Director, who is always available to provide support and resources in navigating the academic journey. Our Academic Coaches work one-on-one with students designing curriculum for each student's unique learning style. Coaches are experienced, passionate, and highly qualified educators with a track record of success helping students improve grades and increase test scores, as well as build confidence and develop valuable study skills that last a lifetime.

As a company, we seek to embody our core values on every level. Our commitment to personal and professional development, a culture of caring, entrepreneurship, and innovation enables us to provide a unique and vibrant place in the education industry. In 2014, Private Prep was recognized by Crain's NY as one of the "100 Best Places to Work" and has been ranked in the top 15 on Inc. 5000's national list of "Fastest Growing Private Companies" in Education for the past three years — 2013, 2014, and 2015.

Our operations span the Tri-State area, Washington DC, and Los Angeles. We deliver a high touch education experience that is supported by diverse and excellent resources in recruitment, curriculum design, professional training, and custom software development.